as cooked on

 TikTok

as cooked on
TikTok

**Fan favorites and recipe exclusives
from more than 40 TikTok creators!**

**With Emily Stephenson
Foreword by Gordon + Tilly Ramsay
Photographs by Lauren Volo**

EBURY
PRESS

contents

foreword

Gordon: When I first heard of TikTok from my daughter Tilly, I thought it was just about dancing and being silly. Tilly had introduced me to it and was already dancing up a storm. Once I saw how much fun she was having watching the videos, I decided to pull back the curtain and I saw how inventive TikTok users were when it came to food—from the viral recipes to the simple hacks to some of the most outrageous dishes I've ever seen. I realized then that TikTok was more than just entertainment, it was creating the next generation of foodies—and still is.

Tilly: Even though I had done fun transitions and dances with Dad, I loved all the food creations I saw. I loved learning new recipes and maybe even taught Dad a few things, thanks to TikTok. I couldn't be more thrilled to see them in book form!

Gordon: This cookbook is full of some of TikTok's biggest trends, displaying innovative cooking and fun dishes to make at home. Nothing in this book is worthy of my reaction on TikTok . . . unless you turn it into a mess.

Tilly: Dad! Be nice; there's some amazing recipes in here that I can't wait to share with some real TikTok chefs. Kidding, Dad!

Gordon: Joking aside, we both can't wait to cook some of these dishes together at home with the family and I'm sure you will enjoy them as well!

Gordon + Tilly Ramsay

@gordonramsayofficial
@tillyramsay

introduction

If you love to cook, your phone has become just as important as a sharp knife. Most often, the biggest influence on what you decide to make for dinner is the people on your feeds—both your friends bragging about what they just cooked and the creators you follow who develop recipe hit after hit (hello feta pasta!).

But it's not just about who you follow. What's made cooking on TikTok so special is the connection. When you post a video of your take on a recipe everyone's making, you become part of the community around a dish—and become a creator yourself. You can stitch, you can duet, and you can meet a ton of other people along the way who also have a passion for great storytelling and knockout recipes.

All those interactions mean that new communities around shared interests are springing up, from cake bakers to air fryer enthusiasts. There's something here for literally every type of cook (and if it doesn't exist . . . start it!). The recipe videos on TikTok range from weekday-effortless to weekend-extra, so whether you love instant ramen or make your own 12-yolk fresh pasta, there's a place for you. And yes, #potato TikTok is a thing. (Tell me you love carbs without *telling* me you love carbs.)

This cookbook is a collection of the most exciting action happening on #FoodTok right now. It's full of talented creators who are making food that's original, fun, and what you want to eat every single day. In these pages, you'll find more than forty creators from multiple countries who represent all ages and tons of different cuisines, and who range from professionally trained chefs to home cooking bosses. The one thing they all have in common is their passion for food and their watch-on-repeat videos.

These are the recipes that they're most proud of and a mix of their fans' favorites, personal go-tos, and trends with staying power. It's a collection of just over sixty recipes—all hits, no skips (and all tested to ensure they'll work in your kitchen). They cover every meal of the day. They're vegan, they're meaty, they're solo dinners, and party food. There's flavors from all over the globe to exhilarate your taste buds. The recipes bring you into subgenres like #steak TikTok, #cake TikTok, #drink TikTok, and more. There are some show-off recipes, but mostly, they're surprisingly easy. Baked oats? They're like eating a cake that took 20 minutes to make start to finish. No wonder they blew up.

> "It's full of talented creators who are making food that's original, fun, and what you want to eat every single day."

How to Use This Book

On the app, you might watch a video a few (dozen) times before you make the recipe. Think of this recipe collection in the same way. Read them through. Make sure you know the ingredients you need and equipment to gather. Look for the #lifehacks to help make your cooking easier, the FYIs to dive deeper into the techniques in the recipes, and I Was Today Years Old to learn about ingredients.

Notice a little extra something on the pages? There's a QR code for every recipe! Read all about them on page 17, then scan one. Watch the recipe's video to see if it might answer any questions you have (like "Is this what I'm craving *right now?*"). Or see how others have been putting their spin on it as they upload their own versions. You might see how someone veganized it, find your next favorite follow, and DM a friend a recipe they'll fall hard for. You might just find your new favorite rabbit hole. Does watching forty-seven versions of the same recipe count as ASMR? You tell us.

Hopefully this book inspires you to make the jump from fan

to creator, too! If you're not sure you've got the chops to make a good TikTok video, check out all the advice in How to Make a Great Cooking Video (page 16) from the creators featured here. Then, choose one of the recipes and "practice" by cooking for your friends and family to get your shots planned and your angles right. You do you. Everyone eating the food you make along the way is *not* going to mind.

When you're ready, post your video with #FoodTok and become part of our growing community.

Don't Be Salty

Salt is very personal: How much you like, what kind you use, how high you like to sprinkle it over your food . . . Many creators in this book have a ride-or-die type, and it's mentioned in the recipe. If a recipe just says salt, then go ahead and use your fave.

Below are all the salts used by creators in this book. If you're cooking with a different salt, use the ratio to figure out how much you'll need. For example, if a recipe calls for 1 teaspoon of Diamond Crystal and all you have is table salt, then use half as much. Easy!

to get the same level of saltiness you need	
Table salt, fine sea salt, or other fine ground salt like Himalayan pink	1 teaspoon
Morton kosher salt or other kosher salt brands	1½ teaspoons
Diamond Crystal kosher salt	2 teaspoons

Iconic

Here's what the icons that accompany each recipe mean:

This recipe is vegan and contains no animal products.

Recipes with this icon can be started and finished in 30 minutes or less.

Lets you know how many people you expect to serve, or how much the recipe makes.

There's a QR code for every recipe! Break out your phone and scan it to see the creator in action on TikTok.

Ming Tsai's
favorite kitchen gear

Ming Tsai is an OG cooking TV star who is now racking up millions of views on TikTok with his videos that cover everything from equipment to cooking skills to must-make recipes.

These are all the tools he recommends for home cooks. Are you ready to level up in the kitchen?

Five Multipurpose Tools

Two-Way Mandoline
I love using this for cucumbers, celery, carrots, and mushrooms!! It creates super-uniform slices.

Knives and Sharpening Tools
Sharp knives are a must in any kitchen. Learning how to sharpen them is also key. A whetstone is essential for sharpening. To hone the knife after sharpening, a ceramic steel or a leather honing strap are also incredible. Both do such a good job at getting the right edge.

Classic Fish Spatula
How else does one flip fish easily without damaging it? The classic fish spatula is key in any kitchen—you can also use it to flip pancakes and veggies.

Cast-Iron Skillet
One of my favorite skillets is my cast-iron. I've had it for over twenty years. Once it's well seasoned, it becomes as versatile as nonstick— you can fry up some eggs, cook a fish fillet or a steak, sauté veggies, or make pancakes.

Two-Grind Rasp-Style Grater aka Microplane
Zest is key in cooking and baking and a sharp rasp makes all the difference. You can use it to grate citrus zest, chocolate, nutmeg, cheese, garlic . . . once you have it, you'll wonder how you lived without it.

And Five Specialty Tools

Sesame Grinder
This is a very specific and great tool to have! It's an easy way to top food with toasted sesame seeds and add richness and nutty flavor to any dish.

Corn Peeler
I love fresh corn. This tool is so simple to use and it works so well—it makes prepping corn a breeze!

Turning Slicer
I make vegetable noodles out of zucchini, squash, carrots all the time. You can also use the tool to make "chips" and to fry up potatoes and celery root for cool garnishes.

Nutmeg Grinder
Fresh ground spices are key for flavor and this nutmeg grinder makes nutmeg snow. It's so cool! You can also use it for small truffles.

Cordless Frother
For milk absolutely, but it's awesome to finish sauces. You can use it to add a bubbly texture and lightness to sauces.

How to Make a Great Cooking Video (According to the People Who Know)

It May Seem Obvious but Choose a Good Recipe

"I believe people can tell when someone is cooking something they truly don't like. Cook for yourself and what your mouth enjoys and people will be inspired to follow your lead," says @theemoodyfoody. So if the latest trending recipe is feeling a bit blah to you, it's okay to pass!

Even better: @renes.cravings and @goldengully both agree that making a dish with a personal story absolutely makes the video stand out. "More and more folks want to understand the person or community behind a recipe," says @lahbco. "Where did it originate, why is it special to you, how can I customize it for my own preferences—these are all questions I ask as a viewer when I watch a video."

Always Be Prepared

Once you land on the perfect, personal recipe, you have to do some prep work. Start with recipe testing, says @chelsweets, since you want viewers to be successful! @rootedinspice has her filming plan down: "During the week after work, I recipe test so I can measure out all the ingredients. Then on the weekends, I film, edit, and record a voice-over explaining the dish or my connection to it." (Another plug for a personal story.)

It's important to plan out each recipe step, says @cheflorena, because there's a lot of editing involved in getting your recipe across in a short video. Even with editing tools, there's only so much that can be saved by cutting! Think about how you want the video to look *before* you start filming.

Get Your Head Right

Every single creator agrees: Each video needs your shining, totally unique personality. Being yourself is what's going to keep your followers coming back. "I get asked a lot of what type of cameras I use, what editing software I use, etc. None of that matters, really. I started with my phone, and from there my personality and hard work has seen me grow!" says @ramenkingivan.

Creativity, patience, and *literal* hunger help, too, says @tazxbakes. (@ballehurns agrees that being hungry is a must-have for a great video; it means you're excited for the food!) And for the @twincoast sisters that means getting into a good headspace before each video: "Your energy is really important! You have to be excited and confident about what you're making because that will show through to your viewers."

Show Me the Life Hack That You Randomly Saw One Day . . .
TikTok is known for game-changing lifehacks—new ways to do everyday tasks like crack an egg, microwave your leftovers, and cut a bell pepper. Every hack that's in this book has been tested (and for that matter, every recipe, too!) to make sure it actually, you know, works. Any time there's a hack that can help you with the recipe, it's there for easy reference. Learn it, master it, pass it along.

Get Your Lighting Right

The food's gotta look good. "Oh my god, when it comes to cooking videos, getting the best lighting is crucial," says @newt. "Better lighting will make food look a lot more delicious, which will then attract more people to watch your videos." And even more practically, @cookingbomb points out: "You need great lighting to show all the details in cooking."

And Make It Stand Out

Another chance for your personality to come through! @cookingwithlynja uses memes (maybe better than anyone out there). @thelucasassis_ loves to sprinkle in education with his recipes. We're all watching food videos to learn something, after all.

"I always try to provide some sort of value to my viewers," says @sheffara. "As long as my content is educational or entertaining for someone, that's all I want." Fun facts, humor, hospitality, good storytelling, dank memes—how will your viewers get to know you?

Finally, Write This Down and Refer Back, Always:

"It's supposed to be fun." @chefchrischo

QR codes

Scan for a surprise: Those QR codes on every recipe will take you to TikTok to check out the creator.

Many of these recipes are linked to existing videos that you should watch, like, DM to your friends, then come back and cook. If you notice something a little different between the video and the book versions, that's not a mistake! Some recipes have evolved as the book came together, and they're (somehow!) even better now. Go with the recipe as written in the book (trust us, they've been tested a lot).

If the link takes you to the creator's feed, it means the recipe might be making its TikTok debut! You can find all of its fans making their own TikTok version when you scroll through #FoodTok.

Lemon Blueberry Biscuits (page 36)

breakfast any time

Family recipe!

**SERVES
2 TO 4**

4 dried chiles de árbol

3 dried guajillo chiles

4 **medium** whole plum tomatoes

¼ **medium** white onion

3 garlic cloves, peeled (#lifehack, page 22)

2 **teaspoons** dried Mexican oregano

1 **teaspoon** cumin seeds

Salt and freshly ground black pepper

1 **tablespoon** neutral oil, plus more for frying

12 (4- to 6-inch / 10 to 15cm) corn tortillas, each cut into 4 or 6 wedges

A few sprigs fresh epazote (optional but highly recommended)

Fresh cilantro sprigs, for garnish (#lifehack, page 101)

¼ **medium** red onion, thinly sliced (Save Your Tears, page 86)

¼ **cup / 60g** Mexican crema

¼ **cup / 35g** crumbled queso fresco

chilaquiles rojos

@theemoodyfoody

Fabrizio slightly adapted his family's chilaquiles recipe while keeping it (mostly) traditional. The one ingredient he never skips is the fresh epazote, an herb with no comparison. It gives the dish that exceptional flavor he associates with special occasions. You can find it at Latin grocers or other markets with a robust produce section. Fabrizio has you make your own fried tortillas. If you don't have the time or supplies, use high-quality bagged chips.

Char the chiles de árbol and guajillo chiles with a kitchen torch or in a cast-iron skillet over high heat until there are just a few blackened spots. Remove the stems, but you can leave the seeds.

In a medium pot, combine the tomatoes, onion, garlic, and charred chiles. Add just enough water to cover the vegetables. Cover, bring to a simmer, and cook until the onion has softened and the chiles are rehydrated and pliable, about 8 minutes.

Recipe continues

Use a slotted spoon to transfer the vegetables to a blender. Reserve the cooking liquid. Add the oregano and cumin to the blender. Blend until the sauce is smooth and thick enough to coat a spoon. If the sauce is too thick, while the blender is running, slowly add in some of the cooking liquid, a splash at a time, until it's the right consistency (Fabrizio doesn't like his too runny). Season to taste with salt and pepper.

Pour 2 inches / 5cm oil into a deep heavy-bottomed pot like a Dutch oven. Fit the pot with a thermometer and heat the oil to 350°F / 175°C. Line a sheet pan or wire rack with paper towels.

When the oil is ready, fry the tortilla wedges in batches, making sure not to crowd the pan (otherwise they won't fry up light and crisp), until golden brown, 3 to 5 minutes. Use a slotted spoon to transfer the tortillas to the paper towels to drain. Let the oil come back up to temperature in between batches.

In a large cast-iron skillet, heat the 1 tablespoon oil over medium-high heat. Carefully pour in the sauce and add the epazote (if using). Cook the sauce until the consistency is thick and smooth, about 5 minutes. Taste and adjust the seasoning. Discard the epazote.

Add the fried tortilla wedges and gently stir until evenly coated with sauce. Divide the chilaquiles among bowls and garnish with cilantro, red onion, crema, and queso fresco.

#lifehack
Crushing garlic with the side of a knife to loosen the skin works great—but sometimes it's fun to change things up. Microwaving the cloves also works: Put the cloves into a microwave-safe bowl and start with 10 seconds. Test, and if the peel comes right off, you're good to go! If not, stick it back in the microwave for 5-second intervals. This hack works great whenever you need to slice or chop garlic but can make the garlic a little too soft to grate.

Giada and Jade's
breakfast croissant paninis

@giadadelaurentiis

On Sundays, Giada and her daughter, Jade, like to turn plain croissants into extra-special breakfast paninis. You can go sweet or savory—either way, these quick breakfasts are indulgent enough for weekends yet fast enough for everyday . . . so get creating!

Slice the croissants in half lengthwise. Add in the fillings (included are some of their favorites, but try your own combinations too!). Press in a warmed panini press until the croissant is golden-brown and warmed through, about 2 minutes.

Sometimes Sweet

- Chocolate hazelnut spread + strawberries or bananas
- Mascarpone (or cream cheese) + raspberries
- Almond butter + pears (and a dash of cinnamon)
- Salted butter + honey

Sometimes Savory

- Smoked turkey + apples + cheddar
- Black forest ham + gruyere (for a play on a croque madame, top with a fried egg!)
- Crispy bacon + Calabrian chile + provolone
- Mozzarella + prosciutto
- Avocado + red pepper flakes + tapenade

A Few of the (Many) Egg Trends on TikTok

Combine the easiest ingredient (eggs!) with everyone's love for an innovative shortcut and you get an infinite number of life-changing ways to cook the first meal of the day. Here are some of the most popular:

The TikTok Breakfast Sandwich

 This bacon-egg-and-cheese sandwich cooks in one pan and comes together with a little creative folding. The cleanup? The dishes are practically done. (Vegans: check out the breakfast sandwich on page 28.)

The Fluffiest Egg, Period

 Why top your breakfast with a poached egg when you could have a *cloud egg*? Bake whipped egg whites in the oven, gently nestle the yolk in the center, bake again just to set the yolk, and put on top of literally any food to improve it.

The Only Omelet Technique You Need

 Obviously, it involves cheese. Crisp a thin, even layer of shredded cheese in a nonstick pan, then add your whisked eggs and proceed. Bask in the browned, cheesy crust.

Honey + red
pepper flakes =
pesto egg magic!

UNDER 30 MINUTES **SERVES 1**

1 slice sourdough bread

1 tablespoon pesto, homemade or store-bought

1 large egg

Salt and freshly ground black pepper

Red pepper flakes, plus more for serving (optional)

2 tablespoons ricotta cheese

½ small avocado, thinly sliced

Honey, for serving

Flaky salt, for serving (optional)

pesto egg toast

@amywilichowski

This is one of those techniques that's been around for a while, but Amy's spicy-sweet serving directions might have had something to do with her version taking off on TikTok. To make them, all you need is 1 tablespoon of pesto per egg (take note if you're scaling up) and diligence so the pesto doesn't burn. You'll be rewarded with crisp, herby eggs and a payoff-to-effort ratio so high it almost feels like cheating.

Toast the bread.

Meanwhile, put the pesto in a small nonstick frying pan and spread it around with a spatula so it evenly coats the pan. Warm the pesto over low-medium heat.

When the pesto starts to bubble, crack the egg into the pan. Season the egg with salt, black pepper, and red pepper flakes (if using). Fry the egg to your preferred doneness (Amy likes over medium with just a little yolk run), reducing the heat if the pesto starts to burn.

Spread the ricotta on the toast, then smash the avocado with a fork over the ricotta. Top with the pesto egg and drizzle with honey. If desired, sprinkle with flaky salt and/or red pepper flakes.

UNDER 30 MINUTES

 SERVES 2

 VEGAN

the ultimate breakfast sandwich

@thekoreanvegan

Joanne—known for her top-notch vegan creations—dreamed up this oozy, toasty, perfect breakfast sandwich for special-occasion brunches and lazy Sunday mornings. And the best part is: It takes less effort than a tofu scramble. Cook the filling components together—a very good nonstick pan is non-negotiable—and add a salad's worth of veggies on top to make it a whole meal.

In a small nonstick frying pan, heat the olive oil over medium-low heat until hot. Add the egg replacer and make sure it coats the bottom. Cook until it begins to bubble, about 2 minutes, then add the cheese and the sausage to the center. Season with salt and pepper.

When the bottom of the "egg" starts to brown and releases easily from the pan, after another 2 to 3 minutes, fold each side of the "omelet" toward the center, with the one side overlapping the other, like an envelope. (This can take a little skill.) A very thin silicone spatula or even an offset spatula works great. You can tilt the pan if you need to get an assist from gravity, too.

Using a silicone spatula or other utensil, gently flip the omelet over and cook until both sides are lightly browned and fully cooked, another minute or so. Transfer to a cutting board and cut the omelet in half.

Meanwhile, split and toast the bagels and spread some mayonnaise on one side of each. Add 1 omelet half to the bottom half of each bagel. Dividing evenly, top with the tomato, avocado, and arugula. Drizzle with balsamic vinegar and season with salt and pepper. Close up with the other bagel halves and serve.

1 tablespoon extra-virgin olive oil

1 cup / 240ml liquid egg replacer

2 slices vegan cheese

½ vegan sausage, cut into pieces ¼ inch / 6mm thick

Salt and freshly ground black pepper (Joanne uses sea salt)

2 bagels

1 tablespoon vegan mayonnaise

½ **large** tomato, sliced (Joanne likes an heirloom tomato)

¼ avocado, thinly sliced

1 cup / 20g baby arugula

1 tablespoon balsamic vinegar

egg replacer + vegan cheese + vegan sausage = ultimate breakfast sandwich!

Joanne uses chopsticks to turn the omelet to get nice, clean folds.

UNDER 30 MINUTES

SERVES 3 OR 4

VEGAN

pomegranate poha

@rootedinspice

Poha—parboiled, flattened rice flakes you can find at an Indian grocery store or online—are a popular breakfast food from the Indian state of Maharashtra. Chaheti's version started with childhood brilliance: She used to put ketchup on hers to get the perfect balance of tangy and sweet. Now she uses fresh pomegranate seeds for crunch and juicy, flavorful bites. Get all your ingredients prepped and ready to go—cooking happens fast!—and you'll be a poha pro.

In a large frying pan, heat the oil over medium-low heat. Add the mustard seeds and fennel seeds and sauté just until the mustard seeds start to crackle and pop, a few seconds. Add the asafoetida, then the kadi patta very carefully and quickly (it'll start to splatter) and sauté for 10 seconds.

Add the onion and chiles. Increase the heat to medium and sauté until the onion is just starting to become translucent, about 2 minutes. Add the potatoes and turmeric and season with salt. Sauté until the turmeric no longer smells raw, 2 to 3 minutes.

Stir in the tomato and peas, cover, and cook over medium-low heat until the potatoes are cooked through, about 5 minutes.

Meanwhile, put the poha in a colander and rinse for 1 minute and drain well. Let it sit for 5 minutes to soften, then check to see if it's ready by pinching a few flakes. If they crush easily between your fingers, they're ready.

Recipe continues

1½ teaspoons neutral vegetable oil

1 teaspoon mustard seeds

½ teaspoon fennel seeds

Pinch of asafoetida (I Was Today Years Old, page 32)

10 kadi patta (curry leaves or sweet neem leaves)

1 small red onion, diced (Save Your Tears, page 86)

3 fresh green bird's eye or serrano chiles, or to taste, minced

2 medium red potatoes, unpeeled and diced

½ teaspoon ground turmeric

Salt

1 large tomato, diced

1 cup / 130g frozen peas, rinsed and drained (they don't have to be totally thawed yet)

2 cups / 130g thick poha (not medium or thin)

½ cup / 80g pomegranate seeds

Sev (crispy chickpea flour noodles), for serving (optional)

poha—flattened rice flakes—cook up super fast, no extra pan required!

Serve with Masala Chai (page 171) for a complete breakfast!

Add the poha to the pan and sprinkle 2 tablespoons water over everything. Cook for 2 minutes, gently mixing occasionally so it doesn't become mushy, then test a few grains to see if the poha is cooked through. If not, cook for just 1 to 2 minutes more, testing often.

Remove from the heat, taste, and add more salt if necessary. Stir in the pomegranate seeds, and top with the sev (if using). Serve hot.

I was today years old

Asafoetida, also called hing, is the powdered resin of wild fennel plants and an ingredient that supercharges your cooking.

A little goes a long way, and when handling asafoetida, Chaheti recommends using a spoon to get your "pinch," then closing the lid of the container tightly right away (the smell is, famously, strong).

SERVES 2

VEGAN

vegan coconut vanilla smoothie bowls

@twincoast

Sisters Ashley and Taylor have turned high-speed blending into a soothing art form, and their millions of followers can't get enough of those smoothie scoops (if you know, you know). This smoothie bowl is inspired by vanilla ice cream, but it's vegan and breakfast approved. Start the night before by making your coconut cream cubes and slicing bananas to freeze. The next morning, break out your powerful high-speed blender for a perfectly smooth end result.

Make the coconut cubes: Pour the coconut cream into a standard-size ice cube tray (the big fancy cubes won't break up in the blender as easily), filling each cube before moving on to the next. Freeze until completely solid, at least 8 hours and ideally overnight. Pop out the cubes and store them in a plastic bag for up to 2 weeks of smoothie-upgrades.

Make the smoothie bowls: In a high-speed blender, combine 4 coconut cubes, the frozen bananas, milk, and vanilla. Blend on high until the mixture is smooth and creamy, about 1 minute. You want the smoothie to be extra thick but if your blender gets stuck (and you've tried the hack below), add more milk a splash at a time. You might need up to another ½ cup / 120ml milk depending on your blender.

Spoon into two serving bowls and top with the toasted coconut. Serve right away.

#lifehack
If your blender is struggling, stop the motor and scrape down the sides, using a flexible spatula to push the ingredients down near the blade. Dislodge any fruit stuck at the bottom, too. Cover and continue to blend until smooth.

Coconut Cubes

1 (13.5 ounce / 400ml) can coconut cream

Smoothie Bowls

2 medium bananas, cut into 2-inch / 5cm pieces and frozen

½ cup / 120ml any vanilla-flavored nondairy milk (Ashley and Taylor use almond), plus more as needed

1 teaspoon vanilla extract

Toasted coconut flakes, for garnish

SERVES
4 TO 5

pancake cereal

@myhealthydish

The pancake cereal trend started when genius TikTok user Sydney Melhoff had the idea to turn those little drops of pancake batter on the griddle into the main event. The idea spread faster than melting butter on a short stack. My's addition to the trend—besides a perfect pancake recipe—was a tutorial video to answer all your questions: No, you don't have to flip each tiny pancake individually! Yes, a griddle is *absolutely* key for pancake perfection (mini or regular size).

In a large bowl, mix the flour, baking powder, sugar, and salt. In a separate bowl, whisk the eggs, then whisk in the milk until smooth.

Pour the wet ingredients into the dry ingredients and mix until smooth. If the batter isn't pourable and is too thick, mix in more milk a splash at a time. Transfer the batter to a squeeze bottle.

Heat a griddle over medium-high heat. When the griddle is hot, melt 1 tablespoon / 15g butter and spread it evenly. Squeeze small coin-size dots of the batter onto the griddle, leaving some space for the pancakes to spread, but fitting as many as you can to reduce cooking time. This should be about one-third of the batter.

Cook until the tops of the pancakes are dry and bubbles form, about 2 minutes, then use two spatulas to stir and toss them. Continue cooking until the pancakes are golden brown and crisp on the edges, 2 to 3 more minutes. Lower the heat a bit if they're browning too fast.

Remove the pancake cereal from the griddle and transfer to a plate. Repeat with the remaining butter and batter.

When all the pancakes are cooked, divide the cereal among bowls and drizzle with maple syrup, add a pat of butter and/or a splash of milk (if using either) and serve right away.

Pancakes

- **2 cups / 280g** all-purpose flour (#lifehack, page 155)
- **2 teaspoons** baking powder
- **2 teaspoons** sugar
- **¼ teaspoon** table salt (see page 13 for more on salt)
- **2 large** eggs
- **1⅔ cups / 395ml** any milk, or more as needed
- **3 tablespoons / 45g** unsalted butter, or more as needed

For Serving

Maple syrup

Butter (optional)

Milk (optional)

Milk is optional—the name "cereal" is about the size—but maple syrup is a must!

Use a squeeze bottle for portioning the batter into perfect little pancakes!

**MAKES
8 BISCUITS**

lemon blueberry biscuits

@jerryyguerabide

Jerry, chef and #CEOoftortillas, couldn't find any recipes to combine two favorites—lemon blueberry pancakes and fresh-baked biscuits—so he did what any good chef would do: He made his own. For the flakiest dough, you can use his brilliant technique to avoid lugging out the food processor or spending 15 minutes cutting butter into tiny pieces.

Preheat the oven to 450°F / 230°C. Line a sheet pan with parchment paper. Put 2 sticks (8 ounces / 225g) butter in the freezer for 30 minutes while the oven preheats.

In a large bowl, whisk together the flour, sugar, baking powder, salt, and baking soda. Use a Microplane (see why it's clutch on page 15!) to zest 1 lemon into the bowl and stir to combine. Add the blueberries to the flour mixture and gently stir to combine.

Coat the 2 sticks of frozen butter in the flour mixture. Using the large holes on a cheese grater, grate both sticks of butter directly into the flour mix. Mix quickly by hand until the butter is well distributed with no big clumps. Add the buttermilk. Mix gently just until well combined—you don't want to overwork the dough.

Dust a clean surface with flour and turn out the dough. Dust the top of the dough with flour, as well as your rolling pin and a 3¼-inch / 8cm ring mold (or a round cookie cutter or a glass with a similar diameter).

Gently (to prevent the blueberries from bursting) roll out the dough with the rolling pin into a rectangle, keeping it 1 inch / 2.5cm thick. Use a bench scraper or your hands to press the sides to keep them straight as you roll.

3 sticks (12 ounces / 340g) unsalted butter

4 cups / 560g all-purpose flour (#lifehack, page 155), plus more as needed

4 teaspoons sugar

1 tablespoon baking powder

2 teaspoons Diamond Crystal kosher salt (see page 13 for more on salt)

1 teaspoon baking soda

2 lemons, for zesting

1½ cups / 240g fresh blueberries

2 cups / 480ml buttermilk

Honey, for serving (optional)

Fold the left side in to the center, then overlap with the right side. Gently roll out again, repeating the process two more times (for a total of three folds) to create layers. Dust with flour as needed to prevent the dough from sticking.

Use the flour-dusted cutter to cut out 8 biscuits and place them on the prepared pan. You may need to gather the scraps and roll out the dough again to get all 8 biscuits (then you can discard the scraps or bake them up as a cook's treat!). You can also use a bench scraper to simply cut the dough into 8 squares if you're in a hurry.

In a small saucepan, melt the remaining 1 stick (4 ounces / 115g) butter over low heat. Baste the tops of the biscuits with melted butter.

Bake the biscuits until they have risen, are cooked through, and the edges are golden brown, 16 to 17 minutes. Remove from the oven and baste with the remaining butter.

Use a Microplane to zest the remaining lemon over the biscuits and drizzle with honey (if using). Serve warm.

The biscuits are best right out of the oven, but store any leftover biscuits in a zip-top bag in the fridge for up to 3 days. To reheat, warm the biscuits in a 350°F / 175°C oven for 5 to 6 minutes.

power up by adding a scoop of protein powder to the blender with the oats.

SERVES 1

berry-cheesecake baked oats

@lahbco

Baked oats aren't a phase—they're a lifestyle. Original oat lover Nasim has always said that "breakfast is dessert and dessert is breakfast," so here's a new way to get some cheesecake-flavor-meets-molten-lava-cake vibes into your day before 11 a.m. But bring it back to healthy . . . ish by loading up on your favorite berries or making it plant-based.

Position a rack in the lower third of the oven and preheat the oven to 350°F / 175°C. Grease a 4-inch / 10cm ramekin with butter.

Make the baked oats: In a blender (or tall container like a jar, if using an immersion blender), combine the oats, milk, banana, maple syrup, baking powder, vanilla, and salt. Blend until well combined (Nasim likes to leave a little bit of texture in his batter). Pour the batter into the greased ramekin. Add the berries and gently stir to incorporate into the batter.

Make the cream cheese filling: In a small bowl, beat the cream cheese with a fork until creamy. Add the confectioners' sugar, vanilla, lemon juice, and a pinch of salt. Stir until everything is combined and the mixture is slightly thick.

Add half of the cream cheese filling to the middle of the filled ramekin dish, on top of the batter (no need to mix, it will sink into the oats as it bakes).

Bake until a toothpick inserted into the oats comes out clean and the cheesecake filling is just a little runny, about 25 minutes.

Let cool for 5 minutes, then top with the remaining cream cheese filling and dust with confectioners' sugar. Serve warm.

Baked Oats

Unsalted butter or vegan alternative, for the baking dish

½ **cup / 50g** rolled oats

⅓ **cup / 80ml** any milk (unsweetened if using nondairy)

½ **large** banana, mashed

1 tablespoon maple syrup

1 teaspoon baking powder

1 teaspoon vanilla extract

¼ **teaspoon** Morton kosher salt (see page 13 for more on salt)

¼ **cup / 40g** mixed berries, fresh or thawed frozen

Cream Cheese Filling

2 tablespoons cream cheese or vegan alternative, at room temperature (#lifehack, page 148)

1 teaspoon confectioners' sugar, plus more for serving

1 teaspoon vanilla extract

½ **teaspoon** fresh lemon juice (#lifehack, page 155)

Salt

UNDER 30 MINUTES

SERVES 1

⅔ **cup / 75g** rolled oats

1 to 3 tablespoons unsweetened cocoa powder, to taste

¾ **teaspoon** baking powder

1 to 2 tablespoons sugar (optional), to taste

Salt

¼ **cup / 55ml** any milk, plus more as needed

1 large egg, or ½ medium banana mashed, to make it vegan

Dark or milk chocolate chips

chocolate-fudge baked oats

@tazxbakes

Queen of baked oats Taz has a method that comes out soft and cake-like every time and a real winner on her hands with this chocolate-fudge version. If you're looking for a decadent breakfast, add the maximum amount of cocoa powder and sugar, and go hard on the chocolate chips. If that's too much, you can skip the sugar and sprinkle just a few dark chocolate chips on top. It's basically oatmeal.

Preheat the oven to 375°F / 190°C.

In a blender, blend the oats and cocoa powder into a powder. (If you don't have a blender, you can skip this step and mix everything together in the next step. The baking time will be the same.)

In a medium bowl, whisk together the oat/cocoa mixture, baking powder, sugar (if using), and a pinch of salt. Add the milk and egg and whisk until smooth. The batter should be thick like cake batter, but if it's too thick, add more milk, 1 tablespoon at a time, until you get the right consistency. Pour the mixture into a 4 × 7- or 8-inch / 11 × 18 or 20cm baking dish. Sprinkle the top with chocolate chips.

Bake until the oats have puffed up and are glossy on the top, and look like a cake, about 10 minutes.

Cool for 5 minutes and serve warm, straight from the dish.

Bake in a pan that will look great on the table—and the recipe doubles easily!

Sub ½ a mashed banana for the egg to make this vegan.

MAKES ONE
9 × 13-INCH PAN

Unsalted butter, for
the pan

Streusel Topping

1 cup / 140g all-purpose
flour (#lifehack,
page 155)

1 cup / 200g (packed) light
or dark brown sugar

4 teaspoons ground
cinnamon

½ teaspoon Diamond
Crystal kosher salt
(see page 13 for more
on salt)

1 stick (4 ounces / 115g)
unsalted butter, melted

Cinnamon Sugar

½ cup / 100g (packed)
light or dark brown
sugar

1 teaspoon ground
cinnamon

cinnamon streusel coffee cake

@zaynab_issa

So soft and tender with the ideal ratio of cake to streusel—this
coffee cake is literally perfect. The cake batter is extra thick,
so if you need a little help spreading it out into the pan, use
an offset spatula to get it *allll* the way into the corners. Bake
it the night before and all you'll need to do in the a.m. is brew
your coffee. If you don't already follow Zaynab for a feed full of
recipes that can only be described as easy-luxe, this one should
convince you.

Preheat the oven to 350°F / 175°C. Line the bottom and sides of a
9 × 13-inch / 24 × 36cm metal baking pan with parchment paper.
Grease the parchment with butter. (If using a glass pan, see the
FYI opposite.)

Make the streusel topping: In a small bowl, combine the flour,
brown sugar, cinnamon, and salt. Pour in the melted butter and
gently mix with a fork until the mixture is crumbly. Be careful not
to overmix or you'll be left with a paste—not crumbs! Set aside.

Make the cinnamon sugar: In a small bowl, whisk together the
brown sugar and cinnamon. Set aside.

Make the coffee cake: In a medium bowl, whisk the flour, baking powder, baking soda, and salt together. In a small bowl, whisk the sour cream and buttermilk together until well combined.

In a stand mixer fitted with the paddle (or a large bowl if using a handheld mixer), cream together the butter and sugar on medium speed until light and fluffy. Add the eggs, one at a time, beating well after each addition until incorporated. Beat in the vanilla.

Remove the bowl from the stand mixer and add the flour mixture and sour cream mixture at the same time. Using a rubber spatula, gently mix to combine (a few lumps are fine). The batter will be thick.

Transfer half the batter to the prepared pan and spread into an even layer (it's thick, so take your time, and Zaynab recommends an offset spatula to help with the job). Sprinkle the cinnamon sugar over the surface, then carefully spread the remaining batter on top in an even layer. Sprinkle the streusel topping evenly over the batter.

Bake until a toothpick inserted into the center comes out clean, about 35 minutes.

Let the cake cool in the pan completely, then cut and serve. Any extra can be transferred to an airtight container and stored for up to 5 days at room temperature.

FYI

You can use a glass baking dish, which heats more slowly than metal and retains the heat longer. That means the sides of your coffee cake might cook faster than the center! So if you use glass, check the cake in 5-minute intervals after the initial 35-minute baking time to make sure it's cooked all the way through.

Coffee Cake

- **2 cups / 280g** all-purpose flour
- **1 teaspoon** baking powder
- **1 teaspoon** baking soda
- **½ teaspoon** Diamond Crystal kosher salt
- **1 cup / 240g** sour cream
- **½ cup / 120ml** buttermilk
- **1 stick (4 ounces / 115g)** unsalted butter, at room temperature (#lifehack, page 148)
- **1 cup / 200g** granulated sugar
- **2 large** eggs, at room temperature
- **2 teaspoons** vanilla extract

Vegan
Pretzel Bites
(page 46)

party
starters

UNDER 30 MINUTES

MAKES ABOUT 18 BITES

VEGAN

Neutral vegetable oil, for the pan

½ cup / 125g unsweetened, unflavored vegan yogurt, such as soy, coconut, or almond (I Was Today Years Old, opposite)

½ cup plus 2 tablespoons / 75g self-rising flour (#lifehack, opposite), or more as needed

1 tablespoon baking soda

1 tablespoon / 15g vegan butter or coconut oil, melted

Coarse salt, for topping

Mustard, vegan cheese sauce, or other dip, for serving (optional)

vegan pretzel bites

@ballehurns

Chill vegan cook Halle uses the endlessly adaptable combo of self-rising flour and acidic (non)dairy yogurt to make these fast party snacks. After the dough comes together, she gives it a basic bath (that's the chemistry term) in a baking soda solution to get a rich pretzel taste. Once out of the oven, you can go the classic route and top with salt, dust with cinnamon-sugar mix, or everything bagel spice mix, or even upgrade the melted butter by adding garlic, herbs, and/or nutritional yeast.

Preheat the oven to 400°F / 200°C. Lightly grease a sheet pan with vegetable oil or line with parchment paper.

In a medium bowl, mix the yogurt and ½ cup / 70g of the flour together until a smooth dough forms. The dough may be very sticky but that's okay!

Sprinkle 1 tablespoon of the flour onto a clean, flat surface. Divide the dough into 3 equal parts and turn out onto the floured surface. Dust with the remaining 1 tablespoon flour.

Use your hands to lightly knead one section of the dough into the flour until it's no longer sticky and is smooth on the outside, then roll it into a log measuring about 6 inches / 15cm long and 1 inch / 2.5cm thick. Repeat with the remaining dough, sprinkling with a little more flour if necessary. Slice the logs crosswise into 1-inch / 2.5cm bites, trying to keep them as neat-looking as possible. (The dough is very soft but that makes for the best soft pretzel.)

In a small pot, bring 2 cups / 480ml water to a boil. Pour it into a small heatproof bowl and stir in the baking soda. Working with 2 or 3 pieces of dough at a time, use a slotted spoon to submerge them into the water for 15 seconds. Carefully transfer to the prepared sheet pan. Repeat with the remaining dough pieces.

Bake until the bottoms are golden brown and the tops are golden, about 15 minutes.

Immediately brush each pretzel with melted butter and finish with a sprinkle of salt. Serve right away with dip (if using).

The pretzels are best eaten hot, but if you've got any extras, store them in an airtight container for up to 2 days and reheat in a 350°F / 175°C oven for 5 to 8 minutes.

#lifehack
If you don't have self-rising flour, mix ½ teaspoon baking powder with ½ cup / 70g all-purpose flour. (The 2 tablespoons flour used to roll out the dough can just be regular all-purpose flour.)

I was today years old

Nondairy yogurts can vary much more in consistency and moisture level than dairy yogurts. Halle uses Silk soy or So Delicious coconut yogurts, which make an easy-to-roll dough. But if you have a different yogurt you like, it should still work for this recipe.

When made with other brands of vegan yogurt, sometimes the dough was super sticky, but as long as you shape the logs with lots of flour and keep the outside smooth, your bites will be 10/10.

FOUR kinds
of cheese!

Frozen spinach
works fine!

**SERVES
6 TO 8**

hot crab and spinach dip with garlicky toasts

@auntieloren

This dip from restaurateur and dance video aficionado Loren is everything you want from a party food: It's decadent, it's dippy, it's cheesy—and you'll want it immediately! Lucky for you, this is a laid-back recipe, and Loren says you can make it with just about any cheese you have in the fridge, as long as it melts well. If frozen spinach is all you've got, thaw it and squeeze out all the water before adding it to the pan with all those other tasty ingredients.

Preheat the oven to 400°F / 200°C.

Make the crab dip: In an 8-inch / 20cm ovenproof frying pan, melt the butter over medium-low heat. Sauté the onion and garlic until soft, about 5 minutes. Add the black pepper and garlic salt.

Whisk in the cream. Add the cream cheese, blue cheese, and pepper Jack and cook, stirring, until the cheeses melt into the sauce.

Add the crabmeat and chopped spinach, stirring until combined. Stir in the Old Bay and cayenne. Top with Colby Jack and transfer the pan to the oven. Bake for 10 minutes.

Meanwhile, prepare the garlic toasts: Slice the baguette into ½-inch / 1.3cm thick slices. In a small bowl, mix together the melted butter, black pepper, paprika, and garlic salt. Brush this mixture over one side of each bread slice. Arrange the bread in a single layer on a sheet pan, buttered-side up.

After the dip has baked for 10 minutes, put the toasts in the oven with the dip and bake until the toasts are golden brown and the cheese on the dip is browned and bubbling, about 10 minutes. Serve the dip hot with the toasts on the side.

Crab Dip

3 tablespoons / 45g unsalted butter

1 small sweet or yellow onion, diced

2 garlic cloves, minced

1 teaspoon freshly ground black pepper

¼ teaspoon garlic salt

½ cup / 120ml heavy cream or double cream

4 ounces / 115g cream cheese

¼ cup / 30g crumbled blue cheese

¼ cup / 25g shredded pepper Jack cheese

8 ounces / 225g fresh crabmeat, picked over

⅓ cup / 30g roughly chopped fresh spinach

1½ teaspoons Old Bay seasoning, or to taste

½ teaspoon cayenne pepper

1 cup / 100g shredded Colby Jack cheese

Garlic Toasts

½ baguette

5 tablespoons / 75g unsalted butter, melted

1 teaspoon freshly ground black pepper

1 teaspoon paprika

¾ teaspoon garlic salt

SERVES 4

1½ **teaspoons** fine sea salt, plus more for the pasta water and serving (see page 13 for more on salt)

8 **ounces / 225g** bow-tie pasta, or your favorite pasta shape

⅓ **cup / 80ml** red wine vinegar

1 **tablespoon** extra-virgin olive oil

Sour cream and onion dip, for serving (optional)

salt and vinegar pasta chips

@feelgoodfoodie

Combine the best parts of pasta (everything) and potato chips (everything else) and you get a pasta chip snack that's a crunch lover's dream. Yumna, who's known for her must-have versions of all the best trends, blessed us with this salt and vinegar version made in an air fryer. While the cooking process is simple, the timing really does matter. So be sure your chips are nice and golden before serving them—you want that just-right dippable crispness with only a *hint* of pasta chewiness.

In a large pot of salted boiling water, cook the pasta to al dente (meaning it still has a bit of chew in the middle) according to the package directions. Drain the pasta.

Put the pasta in a bowl and toss with the vinegar, olive oil, and 1½ teaspoons salt.

Transfer the pasta to an air fryer basket (it's okay if the pieces overlap). Air fry at 400°F / 200°C, tossing every 5 minutes until golden and crispy, 15 to 20 minutes. It's very important that your pasta is golden to ensure the best texture—undercooking won't give you a perfect crunch and overcooking will make them hard!

Serve the pasta chips immediately. If desired, use them to scoop up sour cream and onion dip. Store any extras in an airtight container for up to 2 days.

when pasta + potato chips combine their superpowers . . . pasta chips!

(For a completely different take on the tortilla trend, see @sheffara's recipe on page 106!)

Gabrielle likes to use Himalayan pink salt.

**UNDER
30 MINUTES**

**MAKES
1 TORTILLA**

VEGAN

"cheesy" vegan tortilla

@onegreatvegan

Someone on TikTok dared to ask the question "What if a quesadilla could be more . . . extra?" and the "tortilla hack" was born. The premise is simple: Divide your tortilla into four sections for four times the filling options, do a little food origami, and cook it up until it's golden and crisp on the outside, and full of melty goodness on the inside. Gabrielle has vegans covered with the ultimate plant-based cheesy, mushroom-meaty, crisp appetizer or meal.

Make the mushrooms: In a medium frying pan, melt the butter over medium heat. Add the mushrooms, poultry seasoning, and barbecue sauce and season with salt. Stir to coat the mushrooms. Cook, stirring often, until the mushrooms are tender, 5 to 8 minutes.

Stuff the tortilla: Lay the tortilla on a large cutting board and make one straight cut starting at the middle of the tortilla and going to the outer edge, creating a slit (which will be used later to fold up the tortilla). Spread the queso evenly over the entire tortilla.

Mentally section off the tortilla into quarters and fill the first with black bean salsa, the lettuce and avocado in the next, then the cooked mushrooms, and finally the tomato salsa. Lay the ingredients as flat as possible. Sprinkle the cheese shreds over everything.

Starting with the section to the left of the slit, carefully fold that section over onto the next section, and keep folding the sections onto each other until you have a stuffed triangle shape.

In a panini press or a large cast-iron skillet over medium-high heat, melt the butter. Add the tortilla and cook, flipping and pressing it constantly, until both sides are golden brown, about 3 minutes. Serve right away.

Mushrooms

2 tablespoons / 30g vegan butter

⅓ cup / 25g oyster mushrooms, thinly sliced

1 tablespoon poultry seasoning

1 tablespoon barbecue sauce

Salt

Tortilla

1 (10-inch / 25cm) tortilla (Gabrielle uses gluten-free tortillas)

¼ cup / 60ml vegan queso sauce

2 tablespoons black bean salsa

3 tablespoons thinly sliced lettuce

3 thin slices avocado

2 tablespoons chunky tomato salsa

½ cup / 40g vegan cheese shreds

1 tablespoon / 15g vegan butter

**UNDER
30 MINUTES**

**SERVES
2 OR 3**

bang-bang shrimp

@newt

This crispy, saucy shrimp recipe from Newt is . . . pretty much perfect. He coats the shrimp in panko bread crumbs for extra crunch and more surface area for the sweet-and-spicy sauce. Serve the fried shrimp as is or try wrapping them in cold lettuce leaves. The freshness of the lettuce cuts right through the fatty and tangy sauce.

Make the bang-bang sauce: In a small bowl, mix all the ingredients until well combined. Refrigerate until ready to use.

Make the crispy shrimp: In a large bowl, combine the shrimp and buttermilk and stir to coat. Put the cornstarch in a separate medium bowl. In a third medium bowl, mix the panko, garlic powder, and onion powder and season with salt.

Pour 2 inches / 5cm oil into a large pot fitted with a thermometer. Heat the oil to 330°F / 170°C. Line a plate with paper towels.

Using one hand, take one shrimp out of the buttermilk and let the excess drip off. Put it into the cornstarch and coat well. Put it back into the buttermilk, then let the excess drip off again and put it in the panko. Coat thoroughly. Repeat with 5 more shrimp.

Add the prepared shrimp to the hot oil and fry until golden brown all over (no need to flip), 2 to 3 minutes. Use tongs to transfer the shrimp to the paper towels to drain. Allow the oil to come back up to temperature (no soggy shrimp!), then repeat with the remaining shrimp in batches.

Put the fried shrimp in a large bowl, drizzle a few spoonfuls of the sauce, and toss to coat. Add more sauce, if you like.

Transfer the shrimp to a serving dish and put any extra sauce in a small bowl. Sprinkle the parsley over the shrimp and serve, with the extra sauce for dipping.

Bang-Bang Sauce

½ cup / 120g mayonnaise

¼ cup / 75g Thai sweet chili sauce

2 tablespoons sriracha

2 teaspoons rice vinegar

Crispy Shrimp

1 pound / 450g jumbo shrimp, peeled and deveined

1 cup / 240ml buttermilk

1 cup / 140g cornstarch

1½ cups / 90g panko bread crumbs

2 tablespoons garlic powder

2 tablespoons onion powder

Salt (Newt uses kosher)

Neutral oil, for frying

2 tablespoons minced fresh parsley, for serving (#lifehack, page 101)

Swap crushed Takis for bread crumbs in any recipe! Ideas: mozzarella sticks, jalapeño poppers, chicken fingers . . .

#lifehack on page 74 for using all the scallion scraps!

pan-fried pork and chive dumplings

@diana_mengyan

With their crispy-lacy "skirts"—created by a flour mixture added to the dumplings during the last few minutes of cooking—Mengyan's delectable pork dumplings will impress all your friends. Speaking of friends: you'll need a few to help to eat (and make!) all these dumplings. So turn filling and frying them into a party and then devour your hard work. Or, reward your future self with a freezer full of dumplings.

In a large bowl, combine the pork, scallion greens, ginger, egg, 1 tablespoon of the vegetable oil, the soy sauce, sesame oil, salt, and 1 tablespoon water. Mix them all together with chopsticks in one direction (Mengyan says this makes the filling more elastic so it doesn't fall apart once cooked), then let sit for 20 minutes.

Add the chives to the pork mixture and use chopsticks to stir in one direction again and combine. If the mixture looks dry, add more vegetable oil or water 1 teaspoon at a time.

Fill a small bowl with water and keep it by your work area. Set a dumpling wrapper on your work surface and add 1 heaping tablespoon of the pork mixture to the center of the wrapper. Dip your finger into the water and moisten the edge of half of the dumpling wrapper with water.

Fold the moistened half of the wrapper over the filling to meet the opposite edge. Use your fingers to pleat the edges to seal. Repeat with the remaining filling and wrappers. If you don't want to cook all the dumplings now, see FYI, page 58.

Recipe continues

1½ pounds / 680g ground pork

8½ ounces / 240g sliced scallions, green tops only, plus more for garnish

¼ cup / 32g minced peeled fresh ginger

1 large egg

3 tablespoons neutral vegetable oil, plus more for frying as needed

1 tablespoon soy sauce, plus more for serving

2 teaspoons dark sesame oil

1 teaspoon table salt (see page 13 for more on salt)

7 ounces / 200g minced Chinese chives (garlic chives)

2 (10-ounce / 285g) packages 4-inch / 10cm round dumpling wrappers (about 80 total)

All-purpose flour

1 teaspoon toasted sesame seeds

Black vinegar (optional), for serving (I Was Today Years Old, page 58)

In another small bowl, mix 2 teaspoons flour with ⅓ cup / 80ml water to make a slurry and keep it by the stove.

In a large nonstick frying pan, heat 2 tablespoons of the vegetable oil over medium-high heat. Add 8 or so dumplings, cooking them in batches so you don't crowd the pan (if your pan fits more dumplings comfortably, add them!). Once the bottoms of the dumplings start to brown, after about 1½ minutes, add 1 tablespoon of water and cover with a lid. Steam for 5 minutes.

To make the crispy "skirt," uncover the pan and add the flour/water slurry around the edges of the pan (use all of it—you'll make a new slurry for the next batch of dumplings). Cook, uncovered, until the water has evaporated, the flour forms a golden and crisp layer, and the edges of the skirt start to pull away from the pan, about 3 minutes.

Transfer the dumplings to a plate (it's easiest to break up the skirt with a spatula). For each subsequent batch, make another slurry (2 teaspoons flour and ⅓ cup / 80ml water) and use an additional 2 tablespoons oil in the pan.

When you've finished cooking all the dumplings, sprinkle them with the sesame seeds and scallions. Serve with soy sauce (or black vinegar if desired) for dipping.

FYI
If don't want to cook all the dumplings right away, that's cool— just freeze the rest. Place the pleated, uncooked dumplings on a parchment-lined sheet pan or on a plate and freeze for at least 8 hours. Transfer the frozen dumplings to a zip-top freezer bag. Cook as directed, straight from the freezer. You can freeze the dumplings for up to 3 months.

I was today years old

Black vinegar, also known as Chinkiang vinegar or black rice vinegar, is a popular ingredient in Chinese cooking. The deep, rich flavor and mild, sweet acidity bring complex notes to whatever you cook with it—or dip in it.

Look for it at Chinese markets or order online, and it will store in your pantry for quite a while.

**MAKES ABOUT
30 FRITTERS**

crispy, spiced
fish pakoras

@usajalandhar

This is one of Mohinder's favorite recipes, probably because the fiery, crispy-fried fish bites are super simple to make. If you're tempted to get down with some spicy fried fish for your next party, he says get to your local Indian food store to pick up the key ingredients like besan (chickpea/gram flour), kasoori methi (dried fenugreek leaves), and ajwain seeds—they're all essential to getting the flavor right.

Use a mortar and pestle, mallet, or rolling pin to crush the serranos so they release their heat into the batter.

Cut the fish into about 30 bite-size pieces. In a medium bowl, mix the egg, 1 tablespoon of the lemon juice, the besan, all-purpose flour, salt, garam masala, red pepper flakes, ginger, garlic, chile powder, kasoori methi, turmeric, ajwain, and cilantro. Add the fish and chiles and stir to coat. Cover and refrigerate for 1 hour.

In a heavy-bottomed medium pot fitted with a thermometer, heat the oil to 375°F / 190°C. Line a plate with paper towels.

Discard the serranos. Use tongs to carefully add a piece of fish to the oil. Repeat with a few more, making sure not to crowd the pan. Fry the fish, flipping once, until golden brown on both sides, 4 to 5 minutes total. Use tongs to transfer the fried fish to the paper towels to drain. Repeat with the remaining fish, letting the oil come back to temperature between each batch.

When all the fish is cooked, transfer it to a serving dish. Sprinkle with the remaining 1 tablespoon lemon juice, a pinch of garam masala, and more chopped cilantro. Serve right away.

4 serrano chiles

2 pounds / 900g firm white fish, such as basa, tilapia, or mahimahi

1 large egg

2 tablespoons fresh lemon juice

2 tablespoons besan (chickpea/gram flour)

1 tablespoon plus 1½ teaspoons all-purpose flour

1½ teaspoons Morton kosher salt (see page 13 for more on salt)

1½ teaspoons garam masala, plus more for serving

1½ teaspoons red pepper flakes

¾-inch / 2cm piece fresh ginger, peeled and grated

2 garlic cloves, grated

¾ teaspoon ground red chile powder

½ teaspoon kasoori methi (dried fenugreek leaves)

¼ heaping teaspoon ground turmeric

¼ heaping teaspoon ajwain seeds

1 tablespoon minced fresh cilantro, plus more for serving

2 cups / 275ml neutral vegetable oil, for frying

#FoodTok's Shortest Trends

Two ingredients are just the right amount for a recipe sensation. Here's a list of the biggest trends with the smallest ingredient lists. Scan the QR code to find your perfect version to make.

recipe	first ingredient	second ingredient	why you'll love it
Ranch Pickles	Dill pickles	Ranch seasoning	Crunchy, sour pickles and a hit of creamy, dilly ranch? Your sandwich needs oneof these ASAP.
Homemade Cheez-Its	Presliced cheddar or Colby Jack cheese	Salt	Sliced cheese sprinkled with salt and baked in the oven until crisp tastes just like the real thing!
Vegan Chicken	Flour	Water	Kneading flour and water together (for a *long* time) develops the gluten into a surprising meat substitute, aka seitan.
Oreo Mug Cake	Oreos	Milk	Four crushed cookies and ¼ cup of milk make a cake batter which "bakes" up soft and delicious in the microwave.
Ice Cream Bread	Ice cream	Self-rising flour	Any softened ice cream, when mixed with about the same amount of flour, turns into a sweet bread batter that's ready in under an hour.

#TikTokMadeMeBuyIt, kitchen edition

Leggings, vacuums, pink slime that supposedly cleans everything . . . word gets around fast when the products are worth the hype. With billions of views and counting, #TikTokMadeMeBuyIt is a treasure trove of good finds. When it comes to cooking, these creators couldn't resist some impulse purchases either.

"A binchotan grill/konro, thank you @yakitoriguy."
@hwoo.lee

"Potato starch, thanks to Nick DiGiovanni."
@goldengully (See why it's so great on page 99.)

"An air fryer. I refused to buy one till I saw someone make an entire meal just in an AIR FRYER!!! WHAT!!! I had to buy it."
@ramenkingivan (See the pasta chips recipe on page 50 for one way to use yours.)

"Small kitchen utensils. I wasn't a fan at first, but now I find them to be so adorable. Mini spatulas, spoons, cheese graters, I must collect them ALL."
@newt

"A little plastic avocado holder. The avocado fits perfectly in it, helps the fridge stay neat and organized, and the best part is that they really keep the avocados fresh and green!"
@thelucasassis_

And One "I made TikTok buy . . ."

"I had a video, 'How to Season a Wok,' with over 11 million views. The wok I used sold out immediately."
@cookingbomb

Classic Tomato
Soup
(page 66)

low-key dinners

Mix the butter with more cheese, spread it on the outside of the bread, and let it turn golden and crunchy in the pan!

Pair with @zaynab_issa's Classic Tomato Soup (page 66).

UNDER 30 MINUTES

SERVES 1

extra-cheesy grilled cheese

@shreyacookssss

Inspired by a certain coffee chain's grilled cheese, Shreya's version is so simple it's genius. To make it even more fancy, use a flavorful cheese like Gruyère or sharp cheddar for the filling.

In a small bowl, mix the softened butter and Parmesan together. Dividing the mixture between the 2 slices of bread, cover one side of each slice.

Heat a frying pan over medium heat. When the pan is hot, add 1 slice of bread, buttered-side down. Reduce the heat to medium-low.

Quickly put all the shredded cheese in the center of the slice in the pan and make sure there's a border around the edge so the cheese doesn't spill out when it melts. Top with the other slice of bread, buttered-side up. Immediately cover the pan with a lid and cook until the bottom slice is golden brown and crispy, reducing the heat if the bread starts to burn, about 2 minutes.

Use a spatula to carefully flip the sandwich and repeat on the second side, cooking covered until the bread is golden brown and the cheese has melted, and reducing the heat if the bread toasts faster than the cheese melts, about 2 minutes. Serve hot.

#lifehack
Try cooking your sandwich in mayo! Shreya says it's next level—just mix 2 tablespoons / 30g butter with 1 tablespoon mayonnaise and the spices and/or minced fresh herbs of your choice. Spread on the outside of the bread and cook as directed above.

2 tablespoons / 30g unsalted butter, at room temperature (#lifehack, page 148) or melted

2 tablespoons freshly grated Parmesan cheese (FYI, page 99), or more to taste

2 slices sourdough bread

3 tablespoons shredded Colby Jack cheese, or more to taste

3 tablespoons shredded mozzarella cheese, or more to taste

**SERVES
4 TO 6**

classic tomato soup

@zaynab_issa

Zaynab's secret ingredient to the ultimate comforting soup is the fanciest, thickest balsamic vinegar. That's the good stuff straight from Italy—not the just-okay bottles you'll find at most grocery stores. A little goes a long way and is absolutely worth the investment, because once you taste this soup, you'll be making it on repeat.

Heat a large Dutch oven or other heavy-bottomed pot over medium-high heat and add the olive oil and butter. Once the butter has melted, add the onion, carrot, celery, and tomato paste and season with salt. Stir to break up the tomato paste and cook until the paste has caramelized, about 10 minutes.

Stir in the tomatoes, stock, honey, and balsamic vinegar. Bring to a simmer, reduce the heat to medium, and cook until the vegetables are soft and cooked through, about 25 minutes.

Using an immersion blender, blend everything together in the pot until the soup is smooth and thick. (If you don't have an immersion blender, work in batches with a regular blender and fill it only half full. Carefully puree the soup, removing the steam vent in the center of the lid for steam to escape, and protect your hands with a towel. Return it to the pot and proceed with the recipe.)

Remove the soup from the heat and stir in the half-and-half. If you like your soup thinner, add more stock a splash at a time and stir until it's your desired consistency. Taste and add more salt if necessary.

Sprinkle with lots of pepper, drizzle with more half-and-half, and serve hot.

¼ **cup / 60ml** extra-virgin olive oil

4 tablespoons / 60g unsalted butter

1 large yellow onion, roughly chopped (Save Your Tears, page 86)

½ **medium** carrot, roughly chopped

½ **medium** celery stalk, roughly chopped

2 tablespoons tomato paste

Salt (Zaynab uses kosher)

1 (28-ounce / 794g) can whole peeled tomatoes

1 cup / 240ml vegetable or chicken stock, or more as needed

2 teaspoons honey

1 teaspoon good-quality aged balsamic vinegar

½ **cup / 120ml** half-and-half, plus more for garnish

Freshly ground black pepper

**UNDER
30 MINUTES**

**MAKES
4 PIZZAS**

2 boneless, skinless
chicken breasts
(5 ounces / 140g each)

2 tablespoons Italian
seasoning

Salt and freshly ground
black pepper

2 tablespoons extra-virgin
olive oil

4 flatbreads, any shape
(6 to 8 inches / 15 to
20cm wide)

1 cup / 240ml Alfredo
sauce

1 (8-ounce / 225g)
package shredded
mozzarella cheese

2 cups / 40g baby spinach

easy spinach chicken alfredo flatbread pizzas

@beautifuleatsandthings

**Vegetarians, Andrea didn't forget you: She says you can omit
the chicken and it will still be a flawless dinner.**

Preheat the oven to 425°F / 220°C. Line two sheet pans with
parchment paper.

Use a mallet or rolling pin to pound the chicken breasts until
they're 1 inch / 2.5cm thick. Season the chicken with the Italian
seasoning and salt and pepper.

In a large frying pan, heat the olive oil over medium heat. Add
the chicken and fry until cooked through (you can make a small
cut in the center of one and see if there's any pink inside), 3 to
5 minutes on each side. Remove the chicken from the pan and let
it rest on a cutting board or plate for 10 minutes before slicing.

Meanwhile, start assembling the pizzas: Put 2 flatbreads on each
of the prepared sheet pans. Spread each flatbread evenly with
¼ cup / 60ml of the Alfredo sauce. Dividing evenly, top the pizzas
in this order: mozzarella, spinach, sliced chicken, and more salt
and pepper.

Bake the pizzas until the cheese melts, 8 to 10 minutes. Serve
right away.

The chicken is deeply flavored—literally!—thanks to Joshuah's scoring technique.

**SERVES
3 SANDWICHES**

char siu chicken banh mis

@nishcooks

Joshuah Nishi came up with this recipe the way he comes up with all of his recipes: He takes his favorite dishes and simplifies them while keeping 100 percent of the flavor. Normally char siu is made with pork, but with tasty, versatile chicken thighs in your fridge, you're halfway to dinner. Marinate them with ingredients you probably already have at home, then bake them up until caramelized and sticky. Make the other parts of the sandwich while the chicken does its thing.

Make the char siu chicken: In a medium bowl, mix the garlic, hoisin, soy sauce, honey, ketchup, sesame oil, and five-spice. Set aside about ¼ cup / 60ml of the char siu sauce in another bowl.

Trim any fat off the thighs. Score the underside of the chicken by making shallow, crisscross cuts on the thickest part of the thighs and press flat, so the chicken is roughly the same thickness all over. Add the chicken to the marinade and toss to coat. Marinate for 20 minutes at room temperature or up to overnight, covered, in the fridge.

Make the pickled vegetables: Cut the carrot and daikon into matchsticks (aka julienne) and transfer to a small bowl. Add the sugar and salt and massage it all together. Stir in the rice vinegar and ¼ cup / 60ml water. Let the pickles sit for at least 20 minutes or up to overnight, covered, in the fridge.

Preheat the oven to 400°F / 200°C. Line a sheet pan with foil or parchment paper.

Put the chicken on the prepared pan and bake until the chicken is completely cooked through and the marinade is starting to

Recipe continues

Char Siu Chicken

2 garlic cloves, minced (#lifehack, page 22)

2 tablespoons hoisin sauce

2 tablespoons soy sauce

2 tablespoons honey

1 tablespoon ketchup

1 tablespoon dark sesame oil

1 teaspoon Chinese five-spice powder

5 boneless, skinless chicken thighs

Pickled Vegetables

4 ounces / 115g carrot, peeled

4 ounces / 115g daikon radish, peeled

¼ cup / 50g sugar

1 tablespoon Himalayan pink salt (see page 13 for more on salt)

½ cup / 120ml rice vinegar

Banh Mi

3 French rolls

Mayonnaise

Thinly sliced cucumber

Thinly sliced jalapeño

Cilantro sprigs (#lifehack, page 101)

caramelize, 20 to 35 minutes, depending on the size of your chicken thighs (you can make a small cut in one and see if it's still pink inside after 20 minutes of cooking).

Remove the chicken from the oven and slather with the reserved char siu sauce. Let the chicken rest for 5 minutes so the sauce thickens from the residual heat, then thinly slice.

Prepare the banh mi: While the oven is still warm from the chicken, stick in the rolls to warm up. After 5 minutes, remove them.

Split the toasted rolls horizontally in half, but not all the way through. Scoop some of the crumb out from the middle of the bread to be able to add more filling to the sandwich.

Spread each roll with mayonnaise all over the inside. Add one-third of the chicken to the bottom of each roll and top with cucumber, pickled vegetables, jalapeño, and cilantro. Close up and serve right away.

FYI
That scoring technique on the chicken? Not to be skipped. Joshuah does it to flatten the thicker parts of the chicken without using a mallet so it will cook evenly. It also adds more surface area for maximum caramelization.

Alex Guarnaschelli's tips for pro home cooking

@guarnaschelli

After almost thirty years of cooking professionally, chef Alex has picked up quite a few tricks that have really upped her cooking game at home. Maybe one or more of these tips can do the same for you in your own kitchen!

If you are making something for the first time, however simple, don't be afraid to start by following a recipe. Measure everything, do it by the book, and don't forget to taste as you go (and adjust the seasoning to suit your taste). And keep notes!

When you have free time, make a few sauces or vinaigrettes and keep them in labeled containers in the door of your fridge. This will make weeknight meals so much more exciting.

Good shopping choices can change your whole cooking game. Write a list for the supermarket, leaving the produce part a little open-ended so you can make those decisions at the store based on what looks best.

Having people over? Plan a menu where half is premade and make a large batch cocktail/ mocktail to chill in the fridge the night before. That way, you can enjoy your party *and* your guests.

Weekly theme nights can be really fun and are underrated as far as managing your meal planning. Meatless Mondays, taco Tuesdays, and pasta nights can provide a framework that actually inspires new ideas and dishes.

Make protein a priority. Shelf staple pantry proteins include canned chickpeas, lentils, tahini, and tinned tuna (or other fish). For fridge proteins, I always have eggs, deli meats, and cottage cheese on hand.

Use your freezer wisely! Park a pizza dough there—it's great for baking off and then topping with leftovers. I also like to keep a few breaded chicken or eggplant cutlets and tomato sauce in the freezer; they make a good and satisfying weeknight meal.

no waiting on these tacos! eat immediately!

SERVES 4 **VEGAN**

kkanpoong tofu tacos

@thekoreanvegan

If you need a mantra for veganizing anything, Joanne's got one for you: "The secret's in the sauce!" Thinking back on a Chinese-Korean fried chicken wing dish she loved before ditching meat, she realized what she missed most was the garlicky, tangy, spicy sauce. So she started applying it to literally any protein. Now you can do the same. For the fried tofu, you can substitute cornstarch for the potato starch, but the texture won't be quite as light and dreamy.

Make the spicy mayo dressing: In a small bowl, stir together the mayonnaise, gochujang, soy sauce, and maple syrup and refrigerate until ready to use.

Make the tacos: In a large bowl, combine the pressed tofu, ½ cup / 90g potato starch, and a big pinch of salt. Gently toss the tofu to make sure it's evenly coated. Set aside.

In a small bowl, stir together the maple syrup, soy sauce, gochugaru, vinegar, mirin (if using), and remaining 1 teaspoon potato starch until smooth. Set aside.

Fit a wire rack into a sheet pan. In a large nonstick frying pan, heat 4 tablespoons / 60ml of the oil over medium-high heat. When the oil is very hot, add the tofu chunks in one layer, making sure they aren't touching to prevent sticking. (Work in batches, if necessary.) Cook the tofu, turning occasionally, until browned on all sides, 7 to 10 minutes total. Remove the tofu from the pan and transfer to the rack to drain.

When all the tofu has been fried and removed, add the remaining 1 tablespoon oil to the pan and reduce the heat to medium-low. Add the garlic, chiles, scallion whites, carrot, and onion and cook just until the garlic starts to brown, about 5 minutes.

Recipe and ingredients continue

Spicy Mayo Dressing

½ cup / 120g vegan mayonnaise

1 tablespoon gochujang (Korean chile paste)

1 tablespoon soy sauce

1 tablespoon maple syrup

Tacos

1 (16-ounce / 450g) block extra-firm tofu, pressed and cut into ½-inch / 1.3cm chunks (FYI, page 74)

½ cup plus 1 teaspoon / 94g potato starch (I Was Today Years Old, page 99)

Salt (Joanne uses kosher)

2 tablespoons maple syrup

1 tablespoon plus 1½ teaspoons soy sauce

1 tablespoon gochugaru (Korean chile flakes)

1 tablespoon distilled white or rice vinegar

1½ teaspoons mirin (optional)

5 tablespoons / 75ml neutral vegetable oil

7 garlic cloves, minced (#lifehack, page 22)

2 small fresh Korean green chiles, or seeded jalapeños, sliced

Add the maple syrup mixture and cook, stirring constantly, until it reduces to a thick sauce, about 30 seconds. Remove from the heat.

Gently fold in the fried tofu to the pan, so that the tofu chunks are evenly coated in the sauce.

Spoon the tofu into the warmed tortillas. Drizzle with the spicy mayo and sprinkle with toasted sesame seeds and sliced scallion greens. Serve right away.

#lifehack
Joanne's favorite kitchen hack is taking the root ends of her scallions and sticking them in a jar with just enough water to cover. Give them a few weeks and they'll grow into your very own scallion harvest.

FYI
Pressing tofu removes some of the moisture and helps it fry up beautifully golden and crisp. To press tofu, remove it from the packaging and let any excess water drip off. Wrap it in paper towels, then put it in a flat-bottomed colander or on a plate. Put another plate on top of the tofu, then something heavy (but not so heavy it will crush the tofu) like a can of tomatoes. Let it sit for 30 minutes, then unwrap and proceed with the recipe.

2 scallions, white parts finely chopped and green tops sliced on a diagonal (#lifehack, below)

1 medium carrot, finely diced

¼ medium red onion, finely diced (Save Your Tears, page 86)

8 small tortillas, warmed, for serving

1 tablespoon toasted sesame seeds, for serving

**SERVES
4 TO 6**

baked feta ramen

@ramenkingivan

The story of baked feta pasta (uunifetapasta for those keeping track in Finnish at home) is probably familiar by now: It started out on the Finnish blogosphere, made the jump to TikTok, and took over the world. Ramen-enthusiast Ivan's version works so well with instant ramen, it even took him by surprise. And he's the ramen king! Use less ramen for a saucier dish or if you're feeding fewer people.

Preheat the oven to 350°F / 175°C.

In a 9 × 13-inch / 24 × 36cm baking dish, combine the cherry tomatoes and olive oil and season with salt and pepper. Toss until well combined. Put the feta in the center of the baking dish and gently flip it to coat it with the olive oil and seasonings.

Bake until the tomatoes burst and the feta looks very soft, about 40 minutes.

Meanwhile, after the tomatoes have been in the oven 20 minutes, fill a large pot with water and bring it to a boil.

As soon as the tomatoes are done, put the ramen in the boiling water and cook until tender, about 3 minutes. Drain.

Add the ramen to the baking dish immediately and stir until the feta and tomatoes coat all the noodles. Sprinkle with red pepper flakes and basil and serve right away.

```
FYI
Use a block of feta cheese for the best results.
Crumbled feta usually contains an anti-caking agent
that will make it dry and crumbly, not creamy and
melty, which is what makes feta pasta so perfect.
```

1 pint / **325g** cherry or grape tomatoes

¼ cup / 60ml extra-virgin olive oil

Salt and freshly ground black pepper

1 (8-ounce / 225g) block feta cheese (FYI, below)

4 (3-ounce / 85g) packages instant ramen noodles (save the flavor packets for another use)

Red pepper flakes, for serving

Dried basil, for serving

Put a fried egg on it for a heartier meal.

Use plant-based bacon to make this vegetarian!

**UNDER
30 MINUTES**

SERVES 2

8 slices bacon, roughly
chopped

⅔ cup / 20g freshly
grated Parmesan
cheese (FYI, page 99)

1 tablespoon / 15g
unsalted butter

2 (3-ounce / 85g)
packages instant ramen
noodles (save the flavor
packets for another use)

2 large eggs, beaten

Salt and freshly ground
black pepper

1 tablespoon toasted
sesame seeds, for
serving

Sliced scallion greens
or chives, for serving
(optional)

ramen carbonara

@cookingwithlynja

**Ramen gives pasta a run for its money here with its short
cooking time and ability to be cooked *directly in the sauce*.
Yes, that means more bacony, eggy, cheesy flavors absorbed
right into your carbs. Lynja's version of the Italian mash-up is
flexible: You can use shredded pecorino instead of Parmesan,
or a mixture of the two. Looks like ramen might be winning
this competition. (For legal reasons, this is a joke. They're both
winners.)**

Line a plate with paper towels. Heat a medium frying pan over
medium heat. Add the bacon and cook until browned and crisp,
about 10 minutes. Transfer the bacon to the paper towels to drain.

In the same pan with the bacon fat, add 2 cups / 480ml water, half
the Parmesan, and the butter and bring to a boil. Add the noodles
and cook, stirring often, until the ramen is mostly cooked, about
2 minutes.

Reduce the heat to low, add the eggs to the pan and cook, stirring
constantly, until the sauce is thick and creamy, about 1 minute.
Mix in the cooked bacon pieces and remaining Parmesan, then
season with salt and pepper. Remove from the heat.

Divide between two bowls and garnish with the toasted sesame
seeds and scallion greens (if using). Serve right away.

SERVES 2

steamed garlic prawns with vermicelli noodles

@diana_mengyan

Yes, there is one whole head of garlic that's triple cooked—sautéed, steamed, then sizzled in hot oil at the end—in these noodles that come together easily. If you don't already stock them at home, take a quick trip to an Asian supermarket for the bean threads, Shaoxing cooking wine, and special, just-for-seafood soy sauce (see I Was Today Years Old, page 80) to get the flavor right.

In a medium bowl, mix the shrimp, soy sauce, and Shaoxing wine and marinate for 15 to 30 minutes (room temperature is fine). Reserving the marinade, remove the shrimp.

Meanwhile, soak the noodles in hot water until pliable, 5 to 10 minutes, then drain. Cut the noodles in half.

In a small frying pan, combine 1 tablespoon of the oil and about two-thirds of the garlic and set the pan over medium heat. When about a third of the garlic is golden, reduce the heat to low and cook until all the garlic is golden. Remove from the heat, add the remaining raw garlic, sprinkle with salt, and stir to let the residual heat from the pan warm the raw garlic.

Put a steamer basket or rack in a deep pan wide enough to hold a dinner plate (like a wok) when covered, and make sure the steamer can open completely so the plate lies flat. (Check out the #lifehack on page 80 if you don't have a basket or rack.) Fill with enough water to come just below the bottom of the basket. Cover the pan and bring to a boil.

Recipe continues

Ingredients

- **2¼ pounds / 1kg** extra-large shrimp or black tiger prawns, peeled and deveined
- **2 tablespoons** soy sauce
- **1 tablespoon** Shaoxing wine (see page 132)
- **3½ ounces / 100g** dried bean thread vermicelli
- **3 tablespoons** neutral vegetable oil (Mengyan uses sunflower)
- **1** head garlic, minced (#lifehack, page 22)
- Salt
- **1 tablespoon** seasoned soy sauce for seafood
- Sliced scallions, green tops only, for serving (#lifehack, page 74)

a drizzle of sizzling oil at the end gives this dish tons of flavor!

On a heatproof dinner plate, arrange the soaked noodles in the center, then top with the shrimp, and finally the garlic. Drizzle the reserved shrimp marinade and seasoned soy sauce over everything.

Lower the plate onto the steamer and adjust the heat so it boils steadily but not so much that the water bubbles up onto the plate. Cover and steam until the shrimp are pink and the noodles are tender, about 8 minutes.

Carefully remove the plate from the pan and sprinkle with the scallion greens. (For maneuvering the plate out of the pan, Mengyan uses a tool called a dish clip. If you don't have one, you could use two tongs to lift the plate, and have a helper with oven mitts ready to grab it once it comes above the rim of the pot. Or, work very quickly to transfer the cooked food onto another plate. Do not attempt to lift the plate with just towels, or you'll burn your hands on the pot!)

In the small frying pan, heat the remaining 2 tablespoons oil over high heat until smoking, then immediately pour the oil over the shrimp so it sizzles. Serve right away.

#lifehack
You can cheat a steaming basket by making three bunches of foil the size of golf balls! Put them in the bottom of the dry pot, test it out with an empty plate to make sure it's level, then add water and get steaming.

I was today years old

Widely available brands like Kikkoman, Pearl River Bridge, and Lee Kum Kee all make seasoned soy sauce for seafood—you can find it in some grocery stores, Asian markets, and online. It's a little sweeter and has more umami than regular soy sauce.

the Pasta Queen's
tips for pasta perfection

Your days of blah noodles are *done*. Nadia, aka the Pasta Queen, serves up decadent carbs to her millions of followers, who come for the saucy recipes as much as the saucy commentary. Being Italian—and an excellent cook—she knows a thing or one hundred about pasta technique. Here are her top tips to make sure your next plate is perfect.

Salting the Pasta Water Is a *Must*

Pasta is just flour and water (or egg), so adding a handful of salt in the pot will bring out amazing flavors and . . . your inner Italian! Don't ask me about the measurements of salt to use, I never measure. It should just tickle the tongue and make you sigh.

Pasta and Sauce Should Become One

I dare you to search for pictures of "Spaghetti Bolognese." You will find many that show the sauce sitting *right on top* of bland, sad spaghetti. No, no, no! My grandma would turn in her grave. When the pasta is ready, always throw it in the saucepan and combine them.

Pasta Water Is the Tears of the Gods

Legend has it that the Roman Gods saw someone serve dry pasta and began to cry. The tears were captured to make the pasta moist—and this became pasta water! When mixing your pasta and sauce together, add pasta water and cook a little longer. True beauty will be created before your eyes.

Get the Best Flavor—Every Time

Take the pasta out of the water before it is ready. I am talking, almost-too-chewy-to-eat. Now put the pasta into the sauce, add a cup of pasta water, and let it cook. Then add another cup and repeat. The sauce will absorb into the pasta itself, making you a pasta master to your friends and family.

Finally, When You Look and Feel Gorgeous While Cooking, It Always Tastes Better

True Italian wisdom.
Love, The Pasta Queen

SERVES 4

baked feta pasta soup

@feelgoodfoodie

One of the first creators to hype feta pasta on TikTok was none other than Yumna, aka Feel Good Foodie. Her video starts with this mind-blowing fact: "Because of this recipe, the grocery stores in Finland ran out of feta cheese." But Yumna didn't stop there, she's gifted the world with no fewer than six variations on the creamy, salty, ridiculously easy pasta. The most genius version has to be this hearty, somehow even *easier* soup.

Preheat the oven to 400°F / 200°C.

In a large baking dish, mix the cherry tomatoes and ¼ cup / 60ml of the olive oil and season with salt and black pepper. Put the feta in the baking dish and gently flip it to coat it with the olive oil and seasonings. Make sure everything is in one layer.

Bake until the cherry tomatoes start to burst and the feta cheese softens, 35 to 40 minutes.

Meanwhile, heat a large pot over medium heat. Add the remaining 1 tablespoon olive oil. Add the onion and cook until translucent, about 5 minutes. Add the garlic, and season with salt, black pepper, and pepper flakes (if using) and cook until fragrant, about 1 minute. Add the stock and thyme. Bring to a boil, then reduce the heat and gently simmer until the tomatoes are done.

Once the tomatoes and feta are done, transfer to the simmering pot along with any juices from the baking dish. Stir in the basil.

Return to a simmer and add the pasta. Cook until the pasta is done, 7 to 8 minutes. Taste and adjust the seasoning.

Serve hot, garnished with crumbled feta, chopped basil, and black pepper.

3 pints / 900g cherry tomatoes

¼ cup plus 1 tablespoon / 75ml extra-virgin olive oil

Salt and freshly ground black pepper (Yumna uses kosher)

1 (8-ounce / 225g) block feta cheese (FYI, page 75), plus more for garnish

½ medium yellow onion, finely chopped (Save Your Tears, page 86)

4 garlic cloves, minced (#lifehack, page 22)

Red pepper flakes (optional)

4 cups / 950ml chicken or vegetable stock

1 teaspoon finely chopped fresh thyme leaves

¼ cup / 12g thinly sliced fresh basil, plus more for garnish

¾ cup / 125g rotini, orzo, or any small pasta shape

What are your favorite #fetapasta hacks?

Buy extra feta to use for garnish!

find kasoori methi (dried fenugreek leaves) in indian markets and use here and in the pakoras on page 59.

SERVES 2

butter chicken pasta

@renes.cravings

Rene had the inspired idea to combine her childhood—and current—fave, butter chicken, with the pasta she was craving hard one day, and created your new spicy weeknight go-to. It's familiar and yet totally unexpected. It's also supremely delicious.

Marinate the chicken: In a large bowl, combine the chicken with the yogurt, olive oil, salt, pepper, kasoori methi, chile powder, garlic powder, cumin, and garam masala. Mix until the chicken is fully coated. Cover and marinate in the fridge for 1 hour.

Make the pasta: Bring a large pot of water to a boil and salt it. Add the fettuccine and cook until al dente (meaning it still has some bite in the middle) according to the package directions. Scoop out a scant ½ cup / 100ml of pasta water and reserve. Drain the pasta and set aside.

Meanwhile, in a large nonstick frying pan, heat the olive oil over medium heat. Add the chicken pieces and cook until no longer pink in the middle, 3 to 4 minutes on each side, reducing the heat if the marinade starts to burn. Transfer the chicken to a plate.

In the same pan, melt the butter over medium heat. Add the onions, garlic, and ginger and cook until soft and slightly translucent, 3 to 4 minutes. Add the tomato paste and cook, stirring constantly, until slightly darker and no longer smells raw, about 2 minutes.

Recipe and ingredients continue

Chicken

12 ounces / 340g boneless, skinless chicken breasts, cut into bite-size pieces

2 tablespoons plain whole-milk yogurt

1 tablespoon extra-virgin olive oil

1 teaspoon table salt (see page 13 for more on salt)

1 teaspoon freshly ground black pepper

1 teaspoon kasoori methi (dried fenugreek leaves)

1 teaspoon Kashmiri chile powder

1 teaspoon garlic powder

1 teaspoon ground cumin

1 teaspoon garam masala

Pasta

Salt

4 ounces / 115g dried fettuccine

3 tablespoons extra-virgin olive oil

2 tablespoons / 30g unsalted butter

2 small onions, diced (Save Your Tears, page 86)

4 garlic cloves, minced (#lifehack, page 22)

Reduce the heat to low and add the chile powder, garam masala, cumin, kasoori methi, and paprika. Season with salt and pepper. Cook until the spices are fragrant, about 1 minute. Add the cream and the reserved pasta water. Stir everything together.

Add the cooked fettuccine and chicken, mix until everything is coated in the sauce and heated through. Serve hot.

1 tablespoon grated peeled fresh ginger

2 tablespoons tomato paste

2 teaspoons Kashmiri chile powder

1 teaspoon garam masala

1 teaspoon ground cumin

1 teaspoon kasoori methi (dried fenugreek leaves)

½ teaspoon paprika

Freshly ground black pepper

Scant ⅔ cup / 150ml heavy cream or double cream

save your tears

Of all the categories of kitchen tips, perhaps none is as ripe for hacking as onion cutting. It's the twenty-first century and we're still shedding tears over these aromatics??

#FoodTok hasn't come to an agreement about which of the many (many) hacks out there that claim to prevent stinging eyes actually work—or work for everyone—but a few of the creators in this book have methods they love. Try them all, and maybe you'll shed your last onion tear.

@renes.cravings swears by putting peeled onions in the freezer for 5 minutes before you chop them. "This stops you from crying every time!"

@auntieloren says her onion trick is so good, it's her all-time favorite kitchen hack. "Put an onion in ice cold water before cooking it. It helps keep you from becoming a big crybaby when chopping it." Start by trimming and halving the onion and soaking for about 10 minutes before cutting.

The @twincoast sisters have tried them all but say that if you "place a damp paper towel on your cutting board . . . it does the trick!"

**UNDER
30 MINUTES**

**SERVES
1 OR 2**

shrimp fried rice

@chefchrischo

Chef Cho offers A+ fried rice intel in his recipe for shrimp fried rice—like how to perfectly cook the shrimp and make sure your rice doesn't get mushy. Perhaps the biggest innovation of all: adding butter. Top with an egg fried low and slow, and that's dinner. You can double this recipe if you're serving three or four people, but in batches.

In a medium frying pan, heat 1 tablespoon of the oil over medium heat. When the oil is hot, crack 2 eggs into the pan and immediately scramble with a spatula. Cook just until the eggs are no longer runny, about 1 minute. Transfer to a plate and set aside.

Increase the heat to medium-high and add 1 tablespoon of the oil. Add the scallion whites and garlic and cook until fragrant, about 1 minute. Add the shrimp and cook, stirring, until the shrimp are almost, but not completely, cooked through, about 1 minute.

Add the onion, carrot, and butter and season with salt and pepper. Cook, stirring often, until the pan is dry, 2 to 3 minutes.

Add the rice, sesame oil, and soy sauce and mix. Cook, stirring often, until the rice is heated through (it won't get crispy), 1 to 2 minutes. Stir in the scrambled eggs, then transfer to a plate.

Reduce the heat to medium-low, wipe out the pan, and add the remaining 1 tablespoon oil. Crack 1 egg per person into the pan and fry until the whites are set but the yolk is still runny, about 6 minutes. Slide the egg onto the rice and sprinkle with scallion greens, nori, and sesame seeds and serve.

#lifehack
If you've got any leftover rice you don't plan on frying, here's how to perk it up in the microwave: Put your rice on a plate with an ice cube on top. Microwave as usual and the ice cube will steam the rice but won't melt!

3 tablespoons neutral vegetable oil

3 or 4 large eggs, depending on how many servings you're making

3 tablespoons sliced scallions, whites and greens kept separate

2 garlic cloves, minced

5 ounces / 140g large shrimp, peeled and deveined

¼ small yellow onion, finely diced (Save Your Tears, page 86)

½ small carrot, finely diced

1 tablespoon / 15g unsalted butter

Salt and freshly ground black pepper

1½ cups / 250g leftover cooked rice, preferably short-grain white, but any rice works

1 tablespoon dark sesame oil

1 tablespoon soy sauce

Crumbled toasted nori sheet, for serving

Toasted sesame seeds, for serving

SERVES 6

2¼ cups / 450g short-grain rice

3 tablespoons soy sauce

1 teaspoon dark sesame oil

½ cup / 80g shelled edamame, fresh or frozen (no need to thaw)

½ cup / 20g diced shiitake mushroom caps (stemmed)

⅓ cup / 45g corn kernels, fresh or frozen (no need to thaw)

⅓ cup / 35g diced Chinese sausage or ham or tofu gan

1 cup / 115g diced carrots

1 medium tomato

Salt

one-tomato lazy rice

@cookingbomb

You have Vivian Aronson, known for flexing her cooking both on TikTok and TV, to thank for this new weeknight-saving recipe. It really couldn't be easier: Rinse your rice, chop a few vegetables, and score a tomato to flavor it all as it cooks in a rice cooker. If you can't find Chinese sausage, substitute a smoky cooked ham or even Spam—just don't use uncooked sausage. Want to skip the meat? Vivian suggests tofu gan, a dense, chewy tofu that's pressed and braised in soy sauce and spices.

In a medium bowl or the rice cooker insert, rinse the rice with cold water and drain, repeating the process two more times.

Put the rice into the rice cooker along with 3 cups / 720ml water, the soy sauce, and sesame oil and mix everything together. Put the edamame, mushrooms, corn, sausage, and carrots on top of the rice. (Vivian arranges them in neat, even piles, but you can also scatter the ingredients.)

Using a paring knife, cut an "X" 1 inch / 2.5cm wide and ½ inch / 1.3cm deep into the bottom of the tomato. Set the tomato X-side up in the center on top of the rice and vegetable mixture.

Cook on the regular white rice setting. When the rice has finished cooking, open the lid and season with salt. Mix everything together. Taste and add more salt if necessary and serve hot.

Add more veg!
Like chopped green beans,
bell peppers, or zucchini.

Haitian Jackfruit
Enchiladas
(page 103)

high-key
dinners

Save the ramen
seasoning packet
for seasoning
the ricotta!

**SERVES
6 TO 8**

ramen lasagna

@ramenkingivan

Ivan's ramen innovations began in college. It was only a matter of time before they led to the most game-changing version of them all: lasagna. Think of the ramen as no-boil lasagna noodles with more character. Plus, the assembly couldn't be easier. Use your favorite meaty or vegetarian pasta sauce—homemade if you're showing off—and layer on the cheese. Don't forget to flavor the ricotta filling with your favorite ramen seasoning for Parmesan-like umami flavor.

Preheat the oven to 350°F / 175°C.

In a small bowl, mix together the ricotta, ramen seasoning, a sprinkle of salt, and lots of black pepper. Stir to combine, taste, and add more salt if necessary.

Coat the bottom of a 9 × 13-inch / 24 × 36cm baking dish with a thin layer of the pasta sauce.

Break each of the ramen blocks into thin halves. Fit 6 of the halves snugly in the baking dish. Drizzle ¾ cup / 180ml water over the noodles. Spread the ricotta mixture all over, then top with half of the mozzarella, then half the sauce. Layer the remaining ramen blocks on top, then drizzle with ½ cup / 120ml water. Pour over the remaining sauce (if your dish is getting too full, don't use it all) and sprinkle with the remaining cheese.

Put the baking dish on a sheet pan to catch any potential spillover. Bake until you're able to put a fork in the lasagna and the ramen feels fully cooked and tender and the cheese is golden brown, 25 to 30 minutes.

Remove from the oven and cool for 10 minutes before serving.

1 (16-ounce / 450g) container ricotta cheese

1 seasoning packet from a package of instant ramen (about 1½ teaspoons), such as chicken, miso, or soy flavor

Salt and freshly ground black pepper

7 to 8 cups (1.6 to 1.9 liters) pasta sauce, such as marinara or Bolognese

6 (3-ounce / 85g) packages instant ramen noodles

1 pound / 450g shredded mozzarella cheese

**SERVES
10 TO 12**

chicken 65 biryani

@renes.cravings

Rene pulled out all the stops to bring you a streamlined biryani recipe. The super spicy filling is made with marinated chicken thighs that are fried and blanketed in a thick gravy. That's the Chicken 65 portion—a famous South Indian dish that will have you coming back for thirds. The easier biryani technique was actually developed with Rene's mom: The chicken filling, with a dry-ish gravy for easier steaming, is layered with parcooked spiced rice and plenty of crispy onions.

Marinate the chicken: In a large bowl, combine the chicken, yogurt, cornstarch, flour, biryani masala, chile powder, garlic, coriander, ginger, egg, pepper, turmeric, lemon juice, and season with salt. Toss to coat the chicken. Cover and marinate in the fridge for at least 1 hour and up to overnight.

In a large frying pan, heat about ½ inch / 1.3cm oil over medium-high heat. When the oil is hot, add the marinated chicken and fry, flipping occasionally, until cooked through, 4 to 5 minutes. Transfer to a plate and set aside. Pour off all but ⅓ cup / 80ml of the oil and set the pan aside for later.

Make the rice: Put the rice in a large bowl and rinse 2 to 3 times, until the water runs clear. Cover the rice with water by at least 1 inch / 2.5cm and soak for 30 minutes. Drain.

In a large pot, combine the cardamom, cloves, bay leaves, cumin seeds, and cinnamon stick with 8 cups / 1.9 liters of water. Bring to a boil. Add the drained rice to the pot and boil until the rice is halfway cooked. Most rice will take 9 to 12 minutes, depending on the brand. The best way to check is to fish out a few grains of rice and break them in half to see if the outer half of the grain is soft and the middle half is still solid and opaque. Drain and set the rice aside.

Recipe and ingredients continue

Chicken

3½ pounds / 1.5kg boneless, skinless chicken thighs, cut into 2-inch / 5cm pieces

½ cup / 120g plain whole-milk yogurt

¼ cup / 35g cornstarch

3 tablespoons all-purpose flour

3 tablespoons biryani masala

2 tablespoons Kashmiri chile powder

4 garlic cloves, minced

1 tablespoon ground coriander

¾-inch / 2cm piece fresh ginger, peeled and minced

1 large egg

1 teaspoon freshly ground black pepper

1 teaspoon ground turmeric

1 teaspoon fresh lemon juice (#lifehack, page 155)

Salt

Neutral vegetable oil, for frying

Rice

4 cups / 560g basmati rice

3 cardamom pods

3 whole cloves

The biryani spice mix is key! Score it online if it's not available at a local store.

Serve with lots of cooling cucumber raita.

Make the chicken gravy: In the reserved frying pan with the oil, heat the oil over low heat. When the oil is hot, add the green chiles, cardamom, cloves, bay leaves, cinnamon stick, cumin seeds, and fennel seeds. Cook until fragrant, about 1 minute.

Increase the heat to medium, add the garlic and ginger, and sauté, adjusting the heat if anything starts to burn, until the garlic and ginger soften, 2 to 3 minutes.

Add the yogurt, cilantro, mint, biryani masala, ghee, chile powder, ground cumin, pepper, turmeric, and ¼ cup / 60ml water. Season with salt and cook until the flavors combine, another 2 to 3 minutes.

Add the chicken and mix well. Cover, reduce the heat to low, and simmer until the gravy thickens slightly and coats the chicken, 4 to 5 minutes. Remove from the heat and set aside.

Assemble the biryani: Line a plate with paper towels. Pour 2 inches / 5cm oil into a large heavy-bottomed pot. Clip a thermometer to the side and heat the oil over medium-high heat to 350°F / 175°C. When the oil is hot, add the onions and cook, stirring occasionally, until golden brown, about 25 minutes. Use a slotted spoon to transfer the onions to the paper towels to drain.

In another large heavy-bottom pot like a Dutch oven, add a thin layer of oil to coat the bottom. Warm the oil over the lowest heat possible. Add half of the chicken in an even layer. Add half of the rice over the chicken. Sprinkle with half of the fried onions. Repeat with the remaining chicken, rice, and onions. Drizzle the top with the ghee. (If your pot is particularly narrow and tall, you may need to do three layers.)

Cover the pot and cook until the rice is cooked through, adjusting the heat if the bottom layer starts to burn, 10 to 15 minutes. Serve hot.

2 bay leaves

½ teaspoon cumin seeds

½-inch / 1.3cm piece of cinnamon stick

Chicken Gravy

6 small fresh green chiles (like serranos)

5 cardamom pods

5 whole cloves

3 bay leaves

1 small cinnamon stick

1 teaspoon cumin seeds

½ teaspoon fennel seeds

4 garlic cloves, minced

¾-inch / 2cm fresh ginger, peeled and minced

½ cup / 120g plain whole-milk yogurt

½ cup / 20g minced fresh cilantro leaves

½ cup / 20g minced fresh mint leaves

2 tablespoons biryani masala

2 tablespoons ghee

1 tablespoon Kashmiri chile powder

1 teaspoon ground cumin

½ teaspoon freshly ground black pepper

⅓ teaspoon ground turmeric

Salt

Assembly

Neutral vegetable oil, for deep-frying

2 large Bombay or yellow onions

1 tablespoon ghee

SERVES 4

parmesan garlic chicken wings

@thegoldenbalance

Scroll through Ahmad's page and you'll notice that everything he fries is golden-brown perfection, he knows his way around a meal-making sauce, and he is a master of chicken wings. This is the ultimate recipe because it combines all three. The drumettes and flats are tossed in a light-yet-crisp coating that makes use of both potato starch and bread crumbs. Fry the wings and get lost in the extra-thick, extra-garlicky sauce.

Make the wings: If using whole wings, use a sharp knife—or, even better, kitchen scissors—to cut the chicken wings along each joint between the drumettes and flats. If you like, you can also cut the joint between the flat and tip and discard the tips or save them to make stock (#lifehack).

In a large bowl, mix the drumettes and flats with 1 teaspoon of the Cajun seasoning and 1 teaspoon of the salt. Pour in enough buttermilk to cover (you might not need it all). Cover and marinate in the fridge overnight.

When ready to fry: Pour 3 inches / 7.5cm of oil into a large heavy-bottomed pot like a Dutch oven. Clip a thermometer to the side and heat the oil to 350°F / 175°C. Fit a wire rack into a sheet pan.

In a large bowl, mix the potato starch, panko, remaining 2 teaspoons Cajun seasoning, and remaining 1 teaspoon salt.

Working with one wing piece at a time, let the excess buttermilk drip off (be patient otherwise your breading won't stick), then coat with the bread crumb mixture and dust off any extra. Transfer to a plate. Repeat with the remaining wings.

Recipe continues

Wings

2 pounds / 900g whole chicken wings, or a mix of drumettes and flats

3 teaspoons salt-free Cajun seasoning

2 teaspoons kosher salt (see page 13 for more on salt)

2 cups / 480ml buttermilk

Neutral oil, for frying

1 cup / 180g potato starch (I Was Today Years Old, page 99)

1 cup / 60g panko bread crumbs

Parmesan Garlic Sauce

2 tablespoons / 30g unsalted butter

6 to 10 garlic cloves, to taste, minced (#lifehack, page 22)

1 cup / 240ml heavy cream or double cream

1 cup / 30g freshly grated Parmesan cheese (FYI, page 99)

1 teaspoon red pepper flakes

½ teaspoon dried thyme

4 dry-pack sun-dried tomatoes, minced (optional)

ahmad's tip for the crunchiest wings: let the excess buttermilk drip all the way off before breading to get the best sticking quality.

Carefully add a few wings to the oil, making sure not to crowd the pot (otherwise the wings won't fry up light and crisp). Fry until golden brown, 7 to 10 minutes, then transfer to the rack to drain. Repeat with the remaining wings, letting the oil come back to temperature between each batch.

Make the Parmesan garlic sauce: In a medium saucepan, melt the butter over medium-low heat. Add the garlic and cook until soft and golden, about 4 minutes. Add the cream and increase the heat to medium-high. When the mixture starts to bubble gently, reduce the heat again and add the Parmesan, pepper flakes, thyme, and sun-dried tomatoes (if using). Cook until the Parmesan melts, then remove from the heat.

Transfer the wings to a large bowl. Pour over the Parmesan garlic sauce, toss to coat, and serve right away.

FYI
Leave the preground Parm in the store and do what Ahmad does—grate your own from a real wedge of Parmigiano Reggiano to maximize flavor.

I was today years old

Made from—you guessed it—potatoes, potato starch is clutch for frying. It fries up lighter and crisper than cornstarch or flour and tolerates higher temperatures, too.

It's not always interchangeable with cornstarch—especially in recipes where it works as a thickener—but if you see it called for in a fried recipe, definitely seek it out for the ultimate crispy bite.

SERVES 8

biscuit pot pie

@auntieloren

What's more soothing: watching Loren effortlessly cook the ultimate comfort food, or her throwback '90s playlist? (Trick question.) The real answer is getting to eat her food, and until you get invited to Loren's house for dinner, you can do the next best thing and make her pot pie yourself. It's a creamy, veggie-packed chicken stew topped with homemade flaky biscuits, all super flavorful thanks to herb- and spice-packed seasoned salt in the mix.

Make the biscuits: In a small bowl, whisk together the milk and lemon juice. Set aside for it to curdle.

In a stand mixer with the whisk (or by hand in a large bowl), whisk together the flour, sugar, baking powder, salt, seasoned salt, and pepper. Cut the cold butter into the flour, using a pastry cutter or fork to blend the butter in until the flour becomes crumbly with pieces the size of peas.

Make a well in the middle of the flour mixture and pour in the curdled milk. Snap on the dough hook (or use a spoon if making by hand) and stir just until the dough comes together. Continue mixing on low to medium speed until the dough is sticky and moist, adding more flour 1 teaspoon at a time if it's too sticky to work with, 1 to 2 minutes. (If doing this by hand, turn the dough out onto a lightly floured work surface and knead.)

Shape the dough into a rectangle by patting it down lightly until it's 1 to 2 inches / 2.5 to 5cm thick (the other dimensions don't really matter). Fold the dough over itself like a brochure and pat down again, then repeat one more time for a total of two folds. Using a biscuit cutter or glass with a diameter of 2½ to 3 inches / 6.5 to 7.5cm, cut out 8 biscuits, rerolling the scraps if necessary.

Biscuits

- **¾ cup / 180ml** whole milk, plus more for brushing the tops
- **1 teaspoon** fresh lemon juice (#lifehack, page 155)
- **2 cups / 280g** all-purpose flour (#lifehack, page 155), plus more for dusting
- **1 tablespoon** sugar
- **1 tablespoon** baking powder
- **1 teaspoon** table salt (see page 13 for more on salt)
- **¼ teaspoon** seasoned salt, such as Lawry's
- **¼ teaspoon** freshly ground black pepper
- **4 tablespoons / 60g** very cold butter, cut into small pieces

Lightly dust a sheet pan with flour, then space out the unbaked biscuits on the pan. Transfer to the fridge while you make the filling.

Preheat the oven to 375°F / 190°C.

Make the pot pie filling: Season the chicken breast with the seasoned salt and pepper. In a medium frying pan, heat the olive oil over medium heat. When the oil is hot, add the chicken and cook, stirring occasionally, until the juices run clear, about 5 minutes.

In a 12-inch / 30cm cast-iron or other ovenproof skillet, melt the butter over medium-high heat. Add the carrot, celery, and onion and sauté until the vegetables are soft, about 5 minutes. Add the peas and parsley and stir. Sprinkle in the flour and thyme and stir until everything is well combined.

Whisk in the chicken broth and half-and-half and continue whisking until no lumps of flour remain. Season with salt and more pepper. Simmer until it's thick enough to coat the back of a spoon, about 3 minutes. (If it's too runny, mix together 1 tablespoon of flour and 1 teaspoon water and add the paste to the pan then simmer until thick.) Add the cooked chicken. Reduce the heat to low and simmer until the sauce thickens, about 10 minutes.

Arrange the biscuits on top of the filling in the skillet so that they cover most of the surface. Brush the tops of the biscuits with milk. Transfer the skillet to the oven and bake until the biscuits are golden brown and the filling is bubbling, 25 to 30 minutes.

Remove from the oven and allow it to cool a bit before serving.

#lifehack
Keeping herbs like parsley in a jar full of water and covered loosely with a plastic bag keeps them hydrated and healthy in your fridge. Just be sure to change the water every couple of days. They'll last so long!

Pot Pie Filling

- **1 pound / 450g** boneless, skinless chicken breast, cut into bite-size pieces
- **2 teaspoons** seasoned salt
- **1 teaspoon** freshly ground black pepper, plus more to taste
- **1 tablespoon** extra-virgin olive oil
- **⅓ cup / 75g** unsalted butter
- **1 large** carrot, sliced into coins
- **2 medium** celery stalks, sliced
- **½ medium** yellow onion, diced (Save Your Tears, page 86)
- **1 (12-ounce / 340g)** bag frozen peas
- **1 tablespoon** minced fresh parsley (#lifehack, below)
- **⅓ cup / 45g** all-purpose flour, plus more as needed
- **1 teaspoon** dried thyme
- **1¾ cups / 415ml** chicken broth
- **1 cup / 240ml** half-and-half or whole milk
- Salt

The jackfruit filling is also great on tostadas or on top of rice.

Shortcut: Use store-bought mango salsa instead of making your own!

SERVES 6

VEGAN

haitian jackfruit enchiladas

@onegreatvegan

If glamor shots of Gabrielle's vegan recipes aren't enough to make you want to cook them immediately, the catchy custom song she creates for each one will. Inspired by her Haitian and Puerto Rican heritages, these epic enchiladas are made with jackfruit, a tropical fruit that, when unripe, has a meaty texture that makes it a perfect vegan swap.

Make the jackfruit poule en sauce: In a medium bowl, whisk together the broth, parsley, tomato paste, lime juice, thyme, vinegar, minced garlic, garlic powder, onion powder, maple syrup, black pepper, turmeric, oregano, and Scotch bonnet pepper and season with salt. Set the sauce aside.

In a large pot, melt the butter over medium-high heat. Add the onion and sauté until translucent, about 3 minutes. Add the jackfruit and cook until the jackfruit is tender and the onion is soft, 3 to 5 minutes.

Add the reserved sauce to the pot along with the potato and bell pepper and stir until combined. Bring the mixture to a simmer, then reduce the heat to medium-low, cover, and cook until the potato is cooked through, about 25 minutes. Check occasionally and add more vegetable broth a splash at a time if the mixture starts to look dry before the potatoes have cooked.

Preheat the oven to 425°F / 220°C.

Recipe and ingredients continue

Jackfruit Poule en Sauce

1 cup / 240ml vegan chicken broth or vegetable broth, plus more as needed

1 heaping tablespoon minced fresh parsley (#lifehack, page 101)

1 heaping tablespoon tomato paste

2 teaspoons fresh lime juice

2 teaspoons fresh thyme leaves

1½ teaspoons apple cider vinegar

1 garlic clove, minced (#lifehack, page 22)

1 teaspoon garlic powder

1 teaspoon onion powder

1 teaspoon maple syrup, or to taste

½ heaping teaspoon freshly ground black pepper

½ teaspoon ground turmeric

½ teaspoon dried oregano

½ to 1 teaspoon minced Scotch bonnet pepper, to taste

Salt (Gabrielle uses Himalayan pink)

1 tablespoon plus 1 teaspoon vegan butter

Make the enchiladas: In a large frying pan, melt the butter over medium-high heat. Whisk in the chili powder. Add 2 tablespoons of the gluten-free flour and whisk until completely smooth (the mixture will thicken a little). Whisk in the pureed tomatoes, cumin, black pepper, garlic powder, and onion powder to combine. Season with salt. Keep whisking while adding the broth. Bring the sauce to a simmer, then reduce the heat to medium and cook, stirring constantly, for about 5 minutes to let the flavors mix. Taste the enchilada sauce and add more salt if necessary. Set aside.

In a small bowl, mix the remaining 2 tablespoons flour with 1 tablespoon water and stir to make a paste. If necessary, add more water 1 teaspoon at a time until the mixture is spreadable. Set aside. (This will help seal the enchiladas.)

Heat a small frying pan over medium heat. Working with one tortilla at a time, warm it in the pan until it's soft and pliable, about 30 seconds. Lay the tortilla on a cutting board and top with 3 tablespoons of the jackfruit poule en sauce on the side of the tortilla closest to you. Top with 2 tablespoons of mozzarella. Roll the tortilla tightly, starting at the filled edge and rolling it until it's fully closed (but with open ends). Spread some of the flour-water mixture on the open edge of the enchilada and press the tortilla closed to seal it. Repeat with the remaining tortillas.

In a 9 × 13-inch / 24 × 36cm baking dish, use a spoon or spatula to spread ½ cup / 120ml of the enchilada sauce all over the bottom. Add the filled tortillas seam-side down in a single layer of two rows of six each. Make sure the enchiladas are nice and cozy.

Spoon the remaining enchilada sauce on top and sprinkle with the remaining mozzarella. Top with half of the parsley and half the feta cheese, reserving the rest. Bake the enchiladas until the cheese is melted and bubbling on top, 18 to 20 minutes.

Meanwhile, make the mango salsa: In a medium bowl, combine the mangoes, bell pepper, scallion greens, lime juice, oil, Scotch bonnet pepper, smoked paprika, and black pepper. Season with salt. Mix until well combined.

When the enchiladas are ready, sprinkle with the remaining feta cheese and parsley and serve hot with the mango salsa on the side.

"Sing your song, do your dance, speak your truth, and enjoy the epic enchiladas!" —Gabrielle

¼ **small** white onion, sliced

2 (14-ounce / 425g) cans young jackfruit, drained and chopped (I Was Today Year Old, opposite)

½ **medium** boiling potato, unpeeled and diced

½ **small** red bell pepper, thinly sliced (#lifehack, opposite)

Enchiladas

4 **tablespoons / 60g** vegan butter

2 **tablespoons** chili powder

4 **tablespoons / 35g** gluten-free flour

1 (15-ounce / 425g) can pureed tomatoes or plain tomato sauce

1½ **teaspoons** ground cumin

1 **teaspoon** freshly ground black pepper, or to taste

¾ **teaspoon** garlic powder

¾ **teaspoon** onion powder

Salt

¾ **cup / 180ml** vegan chicken broth or vegetable broth

12 (6-inch / 15cm) tortillas (Gabrielle uses gluten-free tortillas)

2 **cups / 230g** vegan mozzarella shreds

¼ **cup / 10g** minced fresh parsley

¼ **cup / 38g** crumbled vegan feta cheese

#lifehack
Prep a mango for chopping in under a minute: Eyeball where the pit is (it runs down the center lengthwise) and cut off the sides as close to the pit as possible. Taking one slice at a time, slide the rim of a drinking glass between the skin and flesh to peel it in one, smooth motion. Repeat with the other half.

#lifehack
There's a better way to slice bell peppers! Cut the stem off the top of the pepper. Put the pepper on your cutting board with the bottom facing up, then cut along the four grooves in the pepper, down to the bottom. Cut the four sections away from the top, so you're left with four neat pieces with no seeds. Discard the core and slice away.

I was today years old

"Young," "green," or "unripe" jackfruit is what you're looking for, and it can be found canned at Asian and Latin food stores and some supermarket chains.

The fruit has a startlingly meat-like texture when unripe and turns into something completely different (and deliciously sweet) when ripe. Be sure you've got the right kind!

If you can't find jackfruit, fresh oyster mushrooms are just as delicious and meaty.

Mango Salsa

2 large mangoes, cubed

1 medium green bell pepper, diced

¼ cup / 10g sliced scallions, green parts only (#lifehack, page 74)

2 tablespoons fresh lime juice

1 tablespoon neutral oil (Gabrielle uses grapeseed oil)

1½ teaspoons to 1 tablespoon minced Scotch bonnet pepper, to taste

¾ teaspoon smoked paprika

¼ teaspoon freshly ground black pepper

Salt

**MAKES
2 WRAPS**

fish and chips tortillas

@sheffara

It was basically fate when Ara realized there are four components to the classic UK fish and chips and four sections to a folded tortilla (you know the trend!). His recipe is tasty and fun, featuring kitchen flexes not to be missed. That beer-battered fish? Extra crispy! Those chips? So fluffy, thanks to a pretty genius steaming technique. This recipe makes two extra-stuffed wraps and you may have some extra tartar sauce and minty-spicy peas to eat on the side, which no one will complain about.

Prepare the batter and the fish: In a large bowl, whisk together ¾ cup / 100g of the flour, the curry powder, smoked paprika, and baking powder and season with salt and pepper. Slowly whisk in the beer—the batter should be thick yet runny (add a splash more beer if needed). Chill for 30 minutes.

Sprinkle the fish with salt and set aside at room temperature for 30 minutes (the fish fries better if it's not cold). Pat completely dry with paper towels. In a shallow bowl, stir together the remaining ¼ cup / 40g flour with a pinch of salt and pepper. Set aside.

Meanwhile, make the tartar sauce: In a small bowl, mix the mayonnaise with the shallot, capers, parsley, pickles, and lemon juice and season with salt and pepper. Refrigerate until ready to use.

Make the chips: Peel the potatoes and cut into chips (aka fries) ½ inch / 1.3cm thick. Put them in a large pot and cover with cold water. Bring to a boil, then reduce the heat and simmer until they're fork-tender, 12 to 15 minutes. Drain, toss them very gently in a colander, and then return them to the same pot. Cover the pot with a clean dish towel and set aside for 10 minutes. If not frying immediately after, you can transfer the potatoes to the freezer for up to 1 hour.

Recipe and ingredients continue

Fish

1 cup / 140g all-purpose flour (#lifehack, page 155)

1 tablespoon curry powder

1 tablespoon smoked paprika

1 teaspoon baking powder

Salt and freshly ground black pepper

¾ cup / 175ml any light-colored beer, or more as needed, cold

2 cod fillets (5 ounces / 150g each), or substitute pollock or halibut

Tartar Sauce

Scant ⅔ cup / 150ml mayonnaise

1 small shallot, minced

2 tablespoons minced drained capers

2 tablespoons minced fresh parsley (#lifehack, page 101)

2 tablespoons minced drained pickles

1 tablespoon fresh lemon juice (#lifehack, page 155)

Salt and freshly ground black pepper

Let the potatoes steam after cooking for the fluffiest interior!

Maris Piper potatoes are the best potatoes for chips in the UK.

Pour 3 inches / 7.5cm of oil into a large heavy-bottomed pot or Dutch oven. Clip a thermometer to the side and heat the oil to 350°F / 175°C. (You can also check the temperature with droplets of batter—they should immediately rise to the surface.) Fit a sheet pan with a wire rack. Preheat the oven to 200°F / 95°C.

When the oil is ready, remove the cold batter from the fridge. Dredge the fish in the seasoned flour and shake off any extra, leaving a light coating on the fish. Dip the floured fish into the cold batter, let the excess batter drip off, then slowly lower the fish into the hot oil. Repeat with the other fillet. Fry until golden and crisp, about 5 minutes. Use tongs to transfer the fish to the rack in the sheet pan and keep warm in the oven.

Bring the oil back up to temperature.

Carefully add the chips to the pot, making sure not to crowd the pan (otherwise the chips won't fry up light and crisp) and cook until golden brown, about 6 minutes. Use tongs or a slotted spoon to transfer the chips to the rack with the fish in the oven. Let the oil come back up to temperature in between batches.

Wrap the tortillas in foil and put them in the oven to warm, too, while you make the peas.

Make the peas: In a small frying pan, heat the olive oil over medium-high heat. Add the shallot and chile and cook, stirring often, until translucent, about 1 minute. Add the garlic and cook until fragrant, about 1 minute. Add the peas, mint, and butter. Cook until the butter is browned, another minute or so, then pour in the malt vinegar. Cook, scraping the bottom of the pan, for another minute, then season with salt and pepper. Remove from the heat. Gently mash the peas a bit with a large spoon or another flat tool to give them a little texture.

To serve: Unwrap the warm tortillas. Cut a slit vertically from the center of one tortilla to the outer edge. Mentally section off the tortilla into quarters and fill each of those sections with a different ingredient: Start with one fish fillet, then a thin layer of peas, half of the chips, and a thin layer of tartar sauce. Lay the ingredients as flat onto the tortilla as possible—the tortilla will be quite full, so don't overpack it! Starting with the section to the left of the slit, carefully fold the four sections into each other until you have a tall, stuffed triangle shape. Repeat with the second tortilla and remaining ingredients. Serve immediately.

Chips

2 large Maris Piper or Yukon Gold potatoes

Neutral vegetable oil, for frying

To Serve

2 large (10-inch / 25cm) flour tortillas

Peas

2 tablespoons extra-virgin olive oil

1 small shallot, minced

1 small fresh red chile, minced

1 garlic clove, minced (#lifehack, page 22)

¾ cup / 100g frozen peas, thawed

1 small bunch fresh mint, leaves picked and minced

2 tablespoons / 30g cold unsalted butter

¼ cup / 60ml malt vinegar

Salt and freshly ground black pepper

find riblets in most grocery stores and asian markets.

SERVES 6

marinated riblets with guajillo salsa

@jerryyguerabide

The side of #FoodTok that doesn't get talked about as much as the big trends or out-there hacks are all the ridiculously talented chefs serving up four-star food. Jerry's one of them and this is one of his all-time best recipes. Finish these riblets off with a spicy, tangy homemade sauce that's a mix between guajillo chile salsa and sweet barbecue sauce.

Make the riblets: Smash the lemongrass with the side of a knife. In a large pot, combine it with the riblets, salt, ginger, head of garlic, thyme, cilantro sprigs, and 4 quarts / 3.8 liters water. Bring to a boil, then reduce the heat so the mixture bubbles gently. Cook, uncovered, for 30 minutes. Use a slotted spoon or tongs to remove the riblets and transfer to a wire rack fitted into a sheet pan to cool. Measure out 1 cup / 240ml of the cooking liquid and place in a large bowl. When the riblets are cool, cut them into smaller pieces, if you like.

Add the dried chiles to the bowl of hot cooking liquid and let sit until rehydrated, about 10 minutes. Add the minced garlic, minced cilantro, and tamarind paste, and season with salt and pepper. Mix thoroughly, then stir in the cooled riblets. Marinate for 10 minutes.

Meanwhile, make the guajillo salsa: In a large heatproof bowl, combine the boiling water, dried chiles, brown sugar, vinegar, tamarind paste, and garlic. Soak until the chiles are rehydrated, up to 30 minutes. If there were seeds in your tamarind paste, discard them. Transfer everything to a blender and blend until completely smooth. (If your blender isn't very powerful or you just want to be cheffy, Jerry recommends pouring the mixture through a fine-mesh sieve after blending to get a smooth sauce.)

Recipe and ingredients continue

Riblets

1 stalk lemongrass

12 pork riblets (about 4 pounds / 1.8kg total)

¼ cup / 60g Diamond Crystal kosher salt, plus more as needed (see page 13 for more on salt)

¼ cup / 30g chopped peeled fresh ginger

1 head garlic, halved horizontally, plus **8** cloves, minced

1 small bunch fresh thyme

½ large bunch cilantro, plus **2 tablespoons** minced cilantro leaves

3 dried guajillo chiles

¼ cup / 65g tamarind paste (I Was Today Years Old, page 112)

Freshly ground black pepper

Guajillo Salsa

2 cups / 480ml boiling water

16 dried guajillo chiles, stemmed and seeded

¾ cup / 150g (packed) dark brown sugar

3 tablespoons apple cider vinegar

2 tablespoons tamarind paste

2 garlic cloves, peeled

Make the blistered tomatoes: Preheat the broiler. In a medium bowl, combine the tomatoes, olive oil, and thyme and season with salt. Spread the tomatoes out on a sheet pan and broil until they're charred and have started to collapse a bit, about 4 minutes.

Fry the riblets: Pour 3 inches / 7.5cm oil into a large heavy-bottomed pot. Clip a thermometer to the side and heat the oil to 350°F / 175°C. Line a plate with paper towels.

Remove the riblets from the marinade and let any excess liquid drip off, then transfer to a large bowl. Sprinkle with flour and toss to lightly coat the riblets.

When the oil is ready, fry the riblets in batches (otherwise they won't fry up nice and crisp), until crispy and browned, 3 to 5 minutes. Transfer to the paper towels. Repeat with the remaining riblets, letting the oil come back to temperature between each batch.

Transfer the riblets to a large bowl, add about half of the guajillo salsa, and toss to coat. Add more salsa if you like, then serve hot topped with the blistered tomatoes, garnished with cilantro (if using), and the remaining salsa on the side.

Blistered Tomatoes

1 pint / 300g cherry tomatoes

1 tablespoon extra-virgin olive oil

1 teaspoon fresh thyme leaves

Salt

For Finishing

Neutral vegetable oil

All-purpose flour

Minced cilantro, for garnish (optional)

I was today years old

Sweet-tart tamarind paste punches up whatever dish you put it in but make sure you're buying the right kind for the recipe you're making. There's tamarind paste, tamarind pulp, tamarind concentrate, tamarind puree . . . you get the idea.

In this recipe, Jerry uses the paste. *Normally you'd need to soak it in hot water and then strain out any solids, but being the professional he is, Jerry combines that into his cooking process. Remove any tough bits before blending.*

SERVES
2 OR 3

reverse-seared steak

@chucksflavortrain

The Boss of Butter is here to help you master your steak-making technique. Start by looking for a prime cut that's 1½ inches / 4cm thick—you can go a little over, but don't go under or you risk dry steak, says Chuck. His technique works if you're a smoke-enthusiast with a smoker or grill, but it also works just as well in any oven. Cook your cut low and slow, then let rest after the first round of cooking, so you can eat it straight after searing, in all its browned, buttery goodness.

Preheat a smoker, gas grill, or oven to 225°F / 110°C. If using a gas grill, set it up for indirect cooking. If using the oven, line a sheet pan with foil and fit a wire rack in the pan.

Season the steak generously with salt, pepper, and garlic powder. Put it on the cool side of the gas grill, on the prepared pan if using the oven, or directly on the grates of the smoker.

Cook the steak for 20 minutes, then start checking the temperature. Remove it when an instant-read thermometer inserted into the center registers 110°F / 43°C for rare, 120°F / 49°C for medium-rare, or 130°F / 55°C for medium-well. (It will cook the last few degrees during searing.) Transfer the steak to a plate and tent with foil. Let rest for 10 minutes while you heat your smoker, grill, or pan.

If using a smoker or grill: Turn the heat as high as it will go (if your smoker doesn't get very hot, use the pan method). When the smoker or grill is ready, return the steak, over direct heat on a grill, and cook, while brushing constantly with melted butter until you have a nice, dark brown crust, 30 to 60 seconds per side.

If searing in a pan: Heat a large cast-iron skillet over the highest heat, then add the oil. When hot, add the steak and cold butter. Cook, while using a spoon to baste the steak constantly with butter until you have a nice, dark brown crust, 30 to 60 seconds per side.

Slice against the grain and serve immediately.

1 thick-cut steak
(1½ inches / 4cm thick),
such as rib eye, NY strip,
porterhouse, or tri-tip

Salt and freshly ground
black pepper (Chuck
uses kosher)

Garlic powder, or steak
rub of your choice

2 tablespoons / 30g
unsalted butter, melted
if using a smoker or grill,
cold if using an oven

1 tablespoon neutral oil
(Chuck uses grapeseed),
if using an oven

Don't sear more than 60 seconds per side or your steak might be overcooked!

steak: it's kind of a big deal

Have you ever made your way onto #steak TikTok? A place where you'll see so much beautiful marbling, you'll wonder if you're in a museum; where the trending color is always a deep, glistening brown; where people nerd out over the merits of tri-tip vs. porterhouse vs. rib eye; and where you'll find numerous special guest appearances from Salt Bae—yup, he's still around—and the King of All #FoodTok, Gordon Ramsay. If this all sounds like heaven, then read on for everything you need to know to get up to speed with #steak TikTok.

Top Cut

Wagyu: This extremely marbled Japanese beef, with its buttery taste and tender texture, is the cut to buy if you're looking for steak clout. A5 is the choicest cut of the choicest steak, and one that makes a lot of appearances around these parts. A scroll through #wagyu TikTok will have you seeing marbling in your sleep—and figuring out how to budget for a $300 steak.

Top Trends

Reverse Sear: This method has loyal fans who swear it's the only correct way to cook steak so it's browned and crusty on the outside, and tender and cooked exactly how you like it on the inside. Let @chucksflavortrain walk you through it on page 114.

Oil-Poached: A decadent technique that causes a lot of slow blinks: "Cook my steak in *how* much oil??" But the benefit, its fans claim, is that it can make a good steak taste like A5 wagyu (see above). The gist is: Put your steak in a snug baking dish (to use as little oil as possible) and cover with extra-virgin olive oil. Add some garlic and herbs in there, too. Poach low and slow in the oven until it's nearly done, then give it a nice sear on the stovetop. Try it out when you're feeling flush with olive oil.

Must-Have Equipment

An Instant-Read Thermometer: Professionals have mastered the touch test (if the steak feels like a certain part of your hand, it's cooked to the corresponding doneness), but for mere mortals, you'd better get yourself an instant-read thermometer. There are a whole range of temperatures for steak to ensure yours is cooked exactly how you like it—and usually the difference between them is a mere 10°F / 5°C.

Rare: 120° to 125°F / 49° to 52°C
Medium-Rare: 126° to 135°F / 52° to 57°C
Medium: 136° to 145°F / 57° to 63°C
Medium-Well: 146° to 155°F / 63° to 68°C
Well: (why bother)

A Cast-Iron Skillet: To get that glorious steak browning and crusty as quickly as possible (especially for the reverse sear method), you need a rippin' hot pan. Cast iron heats up slowly but retains heat so well that you can get that close-up-worthy crust in as little as 30 seconds a side.

If you can't find dried Mexican marjoram, use any marjoram.

SERVES 8

beef short rib birria "super crunk wrap"

@hwoo.lee

Birria is spicy, braised beef (or sometimes goat) said to have originated in the Mexican state of Jalisco and turned into a taco in Tijuana. Chef h woo takes the birria trend to the next level with wraps stuffed with short ribs, pickled onions, crispy tostadas, and . . . okay, stop reading and make it. You can, of course, sub in store-bought flour tortillas to save time; you can also start and end with making the birria and serve it with the broth, chopped fresh cilantro, and sweet onions.

Make the short rib birria: In a small frying pan, cook the chiles over medium-high heat, turning them often with tongs, until toasted and fragrant but not blackened or burnt, 2 to 3 minutes. Transfer the chiles to a heatproof medium bowl and cover with boiling water. Let soak for 30 minutes. Drain the chiles and transfer to a blender (discard the soaking water).

Season the short ribs on all sides with salt and pepper. In a large frying pan, heat the oil over medium-high heat. When the oil is hot, add the short ribs and sear until each side is golden brown, about 1 minute per side. Remove the short ribs and place in a large Dutch oven or other ovenproof pot. Do not clean the frying pan.

Return the pan to medium-high heat. Add the tomatoes, onion, and garlic and cook, scraping the bottom of the pan with a spatula, until the vegetables are softened and browned, 4 to 5 minutes. Transfer the vegetables to the blender.

Recipe and ingredients continue

Short Rib Birria

5 dried California chiles, stemmed and seeded

Boiling water

3 pounds / 1.4kg beef short ribs

Salt and freshly ground black pepper (h woo uses fine sea salt)

1 tablespoon neutral vegetable oil

5 medium plum tomatoes, quartered

1 small white onion, quartered

4 garlic cloves, peeled

12 black peppercorns

5 whole cloves

½ teaspoon cumin seeds

½ cup / 120ml distilled white vinegar

1-inch / 2.5cm piece fresh ginger, peeled

1 stick cinnamon, preferably Mexican

1 tablespoon achiote paste (I Was Today Years Old, page 121)

1 teaspoon dried oregano, preferably Mexican

½ teaspoon dried marjoram, preferably Mexican

4 cups / 960ml chicken or beef stock

In a small frying pan, toast the peppercorns, cloves, and cumin seeds over medium-high heat, stirring often, until fragrant, 1 to 2 minutes. Transfer the spices to the blender with the vegetables.

Add the vinegar, ginger, cinnamon, achiote paste, oregano, and marjoram to the blender and blend on high until smooth. Pour the puree over the short ribs, toss to coat, then cover and let marinate in the fridge for at least 4 hours, preferably overnight.

Arrange the oven racks so the covered Dutch oven can fit, then preheat the oven to 350°F / 175°C.

Remove the Dutch oven with the short ribs from the fridge and transfer to the oven (straight from the fridge is fine). Bake, covered, until the meat is fork-tender and the seasoning puree is thickened, 3 to 4 hours, starting to check after about 2½ hours.

To make the broth, transfer the Dutch oven with short ribs to a burner over low heat. Pour in enough chicken stock to completely submerge the meat (you might not need all of it). Simmer uncovered for 30 minutes, stirring occasionally, to let the flavors combine. The meat will absorb some of the stock (sometimes up to half of it) while it simmers, that's fine!

Shred the meat and proceed with the recipe, or let it cool in the pot with the broth, then store covered in an airtight container in the fridge for up to 4 days, reheating what you need.

Make the pickled red onions: Put the sliced onion into a large heatproof bowl. In a medium saucepan, combine the cider vinegar, white vinegar, hibiscus flowers (if using), honey, salt, pepper flakes, and 4 cups / 960ml water. Bring the mixture to a boil over high heat. Once it comes to a boil, remove from the heat. Using a fine-mesh sieve, pour the liquid over the onion (discard the solids). Let the mixture cool to room temperature. If not using right away, put the onions and pickling liquid in an airtight container to store in the fridge for up to 2 weeks.

Make the flour tortillas: In a large bowl, mix the flour, lard, salt, and baking powder until coarse crumbs form. Add the warm water and knead until a ball forms, about 1 minute. Divide the dough into 8 equal pieces. Wrap each with plastic or put them back in the bowl, making sure they don't touch. Cover and let rest for 20 minutes.

After the tortilla dough has rested, dust your work surface lightly with flour. Using a rolling pin, roll out one dough ball to a round 9 inches / 23cm in diameter and ¼ inch / 6mm thick. Repeat with the remaining dough balls to make 8 tortillas, dusting with more flour as needed.

Pickled Red Onions

1 large red onion, thinly sliced (Save Your Tears, page 86)

½ cup / 120ml apple cider vinegar

½ cup / 120ml distilled white vinegar

¼ cup / 8g dried hibiscus flowers (optional)

3 tablespoons honey

3 tablespoons fine sea salt

¼ teaspoon red pepper flakes

Flour Tortillas

2 cups / 280g all-purpose flour (#lifehack, page 155), plus more for rolling

¼ cup / 45g pork lard

1 teaspoon fine sea salt

½ teaspoon baking powder

⅔ cup / 160ml warm water

Heat a large frying pan over medium-high heat. When the pan is hot, add a tortilla and cook until browned in spots and cooked through, about 45 seconds per side. Keep the finished tortilla covered with a towel and repeat with the remaining dough.

Make the crunk wraps: Place one tortilla on a flat surface. Put ½ cup / 75g shredded birria in the center 4 inches / 10cm of the tortilla, then top with ¼ cup / 25g queso Oaxaca, 1 tostada, 2 tablespoons crema, ¼ cup / 8g romaine lettuce, some tomatoes, pickled onions, and cilantro. Fold the tortilla's edges in over the filling to make a package. Repeat with the remaining ingredients.

Heat a large frying pan over medium heat. When the pan is hot, carefully add one wrap, sealed-side down, and cook until golden brown, 1 to 2 minutes. Flip the wrap and repeat on the other side. Slide the wrap onto a serving plate and repeat with the remaining wraps.

Serve with lime wedges and a side of hot birria broth for dipping (if using).

Crunk Wraps

- **2 cups / 200g** queso Oaxaca, thinly sliced
- **8** fried tostadas (about 6 inches / 15cm in diameter)
- **1 cup / 240g** Mexican crema
- **2 cups / 65g** thinly sliced romaine lettuce
- **3 medium** plum tomatoes, diced
- Minced fresh cilantro (#lifehack, page 101)
- Lime wedges, for serving
- Birria broth, warmed (optional)

I was today years old

To get the birria flavor just right, you've got to use achiote paste.

Achiote paste is a thick seasoning mix whose main ingredient is annatto seed (aka achiote), which gives it a stunning, red-orange color. The paste also includes a mix of spices (that varies by brand, cook, and region), garlic, sometimes chiles, and often citrus like orange zest or Seville orange juice.

You can find it in a grocery store next to other Mexican ingredients.

*Grilled Jalapeño
Corn Off the Cob
(page 128)*

eat your veggies

Admire those cheese pulls!

**UNDER
30 MINUTES**

SERVES 2

1 (15-ounce / 425g) can
corn kernels, drained
and rinsed

2 tablespoons
mayonnaise

1½ teaspoons sugar

Salt and freshly ground
black pepper

1 tablespoon / 15g
unsalted butter

½ cup / 60g shredded
mozzarella cheese

korean corn cheese

@chefchrischo

**Chef Cho, known for his fun and easy Korean cooking videos,
created his version of this comfort food classic based on
childhood memories. It's simple enough to whip up for any
meal, and also makes a great late-night snack (if you know
you know).**

In a medium bowl, combine the corn, mayonnaise, and sugar and
season with salt and pepper. Mix to coat the corn.

Heat a small nonstick frying pan over high heat. When the pan
is hot, add the butter and corn mixture and cook until the corn is
sizzling, 1 to 2 minutes.

Sprinkle the mozzarella evenly over the corn, then cover with a lid
and cook until the cheese melts, 1 to 2 minutes. Bring the pan to
the table and serve right away.

be a lover.
not a hater.

Boil-dry-smash-crisp-eat!

**SERVES
2 TO 4**

VEGAN

sweet chile-smashed sprouts

@ballehurns

Brussels sprouts turn out-of-this-world when caramelized over high heat. Halle's version is everything you want in a veggie side: It's full of spicy sweet flavors that pair with tons of different dishes and uses pantry basics. Just be sure to not overcook the veggies while steaming and pat them bone-dry before roasting. Moisture is the enemy of a good, crisp sprout.

Preheat the oven to 450°F / 230°C. Line a sheet pan with parchment paper.

Fill a large bowl with ice water. Put a steaming basket or heatproof colander in a pot that it will fit in securely and can be covered steaming. (Or see the steamer #lifehack on page 80.) Fill the pot so the water comes just below the bottom of the steamer.

Bring the water to a simmer. Add the Brussels sprouts to the steamer, cover, and steam until a sharp knife can be inserted easily into the sprouts, 15 to 20 minutes. (Check the water level occasionally so the pot doesn't boil dry.)

Transfer the Brussels sprouts to the ice bath. When they are cool, drain. Use a towel to thoroughly dry the sprouts.

In a medium bowl, mix the olive oil, maple syrup, soy sauce, sriracha, garlic, onion powder, and pepper and season with salt. Add the sprouts and stir to coat. Use tongs to transfer the sprouts to the lined sheet pan, reserving the extra sauce in the bowl. Using the bottom of a sturdy cup, firmly press down on each sprout until it's about ½ inch / 1.3cm thick. Make sure they don't touch.

Bake until the sauce has caramelized and the bottoms of the sprouts are crisp, 15 to 20 minutes. Transfer the sprouts to a serving dish, drizzle with the reserved sauce, and serve.

8 ounces / 225g Brussels sprouts, trimmed and left whole

¼ cup / 60ml extra-virgin olive oil

1 tablespoon maple syrup

1 tablespoon soy sauce

1 tablespoon sriracha

1 garlic clove, minced (#lifehack, page 22)

½ teaspoon onion powder

½ teaspoon freshly ground black pepper

Salt (Halle uses coarse ground)

UNDER 30 MINUTES

SERVES 4 TO 6

grilled jalapeño corn off the cob

@cookingwithshereen

Shereen is known for her next-level cooking from scratch, like this quick side to make all summer long. Here's what you need to know: The corn, it's gotta be fresh. The jalapeños, they gotta be spicy (leave those seeds in!). The dairy, it's gotta be thicc. If you don't have crema, you can swap in mascarpone or crème fraîche. Just don't use sour cream, or your sauce will be so sad and broken.

Heat a gas grill to medium heat. Brush a thin, even layer of oil on the corn. When the grill is hot, add the corn, then lower the lid and grill, turning occasionally and lowering the heat if the corn starts to burn, until evenly charred, about 8 minutes.

Transfer the corn to a sheet pan and when cool enough to handle, cut the kernels off the cob. (Shereen's chefie tip: Place a small folded towel on the sheet pan and stand the corn upright on the towel, so it doesn't slip while cutting the kernels off the cob. Cut the kernels from top to bottom, turning the cob as you go.)

In a large frying pan, melt the butter over medium heat. Add the minced jalapeño and sauté until slightly soft, about 1 minute. Reduce the heat to medium-low and stir in the corn kernels. Add the pepper, season with salt, and cook, tossing occasionally, until the corn is warmed through, 1 to 2 minutes.

Reduce the heat to low, stir in the crema, and keep stirring constantly for 30 seconds. Remove from the heat (to keep the sauce smooth and emulsified—don't break the sauce!) and continue stirring until fully blended.

Stir in the cilantro and transfer to a serving bowl. Garnish with the sliced jalapeño, cilantro, and lime wedges for squeezing over the corn.

Neutral vegetable oil (Shereen uses avocado oil)

6 ears corn, shucked (leave a bit of the end attached for a handle!)

6 tablespoons / 85g unsalted butter

2 small jalapeños, 1 minced and 1 thinly sliced crosswise (or 1 large, half minced and half sliced)

½ teaspoon freshly ground black pepper

Salt (Shereen uses kosher)

⅓ cup / 80g Mexican crema, mascarpone, or crème fraîche

¼ cup / 10g minced fresh cilantro (#lifehack, page 101), plus more for serving

1 lime, cut into wedges, for serving

"because you're fancy!"

If you hear the corn pop while grilling, don't worry, it does that!

**UNDER
30 MINUTES**

SERVES 4

Sauce

2 tablespoons soy sauce

1 tablespoon black vinegar (I Was Today Years Old, page 58)

1 teaspoon cornstarch

1 teaspoon sugar

Salt

Cabbage

1 pound / 450g Taiwanese flat cabbage (about ½ medium head) or other cabbage

5 ounces / 140g sliced bacon (5 or 6 slices), cut into 1-inch / 2.5cm pieces

6 small dried Sichuan chiles (see page 132)

½ teaspoon red Sichuan peppercorns (see page 132)

5 garlic cloves, lightly crushed (#lifehack, page 22)

hand-pulled cabbage with bacon

@cookingbomb

Hot, sour, and slightly sweet sauce gets acquainted with smoky bacon in this twist on a classic Sichuan dish. It's traditionally made with chopped fresh pork belly, but when Vivian Aronson moved to the United States, bacon was easier to find, so she rolled with it. Taiwanese flat cabbage is a squat, large variety with loosely packed leaves that are easy to tear (the most fun part of the recipe).

Make the sauce: In a small bowl, mix the soy sauce, vinegar, cornstarch, sugar, and 1 tablespoon water. Season with salt.

Make the cabbage: Rip the leaves into square pieces about 3 inches / 7.5cm wide (it's fine if some are smaller). Make sure the cabbage is completely dry so it won't splatter in the pan.

Heat a large well-seasoned wok over medium heat. Add ¼ cup / 60ml water and the bacon. Cook until the bacon is crispy, reducing the heat a bit if your stove is strong and the bacon starts to burn, 4 to 6 minutes. Remove the bacon with a slotted spoon and transfer to a plate. Leave the fat in the pan.

Raise the heat to medium-high. When the bacon fat smokes, add the chiles and Sichuan peppercorns. Stir-fry for about 20 seconds, add the garlic, and stir-fry until fragrant, a few seconds.

Add the cabbage and stir-fry until the cabbage is wilted but still crunchy, about 3 minutes. Add the sauce and bacon and stir-fry just until the sauce is heated through, about 20 seconds. Transfer the cabbage to a serving dish and serve right away.

A large cast-iron skillet is a good sub for a wok.

Any cabbage works (this is Napa) but flat cabbage has the best texture!

pantry goals
with The Woks of Life

@thewoksoflife

Obsessed with this new way to cook cabbage on page 130? Same. Now that you've got some essential Chinese ingredients on hand, there are so many recipes that you can make. We got the lowdown on these ingredients (plus a few more) from The Woks of Life, a super talented family of cooks.

1. Soy Sauce (Light & Dark)

We use a Chinese light soy sauce most often. A good soy sauce will always be naturally brewed and made with water, soybeans, wheat flour, and salt. Dark soy sauce is thicker and richer than light soy sauce—a small spoonful can transform the color of a dish.

2. Toasted Sesame Oil

Sesame oil has a deep nutty flavor and dark, rich color thanks to the toasted sesame seeds. Used as a seasoning rather than a cooking oil, just a little works wonders.

3. Shaoxing Wine

Shaoxing wine may just be our secret MVP of cooking. The salted version of this rice wine for cooking is the most common (and affordable).

4. Oyster Sauce

Our grandpa (Bill's father), a career Chinese chef, always said, "If you want to make a dish taste better, just add oyster sauce." Why? It's a shortcut to a rich layer of flavor that's not at all fishy.

5. Ground White Pepper

White pepper is just black pepper with the outer husk removed! It'll give you a steady burn at the back of the throat—think warming rather than spicy like a hot chili pepper.

6. Whole Dried Sichuan Chiles

These are irreplaceable. Period! They have a bright red color, moderate heat, and intense flavor. Go-to varieties are "Facing Heaven" chiles, "Bullet Head" chiles, and the longer curved Er Jing Tiao chiles.

7. Red Sichuan Peppercorns

Sichuan peppercorns are part of the beloved regional flavor known as "mala," or "numbing-spicy." In small quantities, there's no numbing effect, just extra flavor.

8. Garlic, Ginger, and Scallions

Okay, so this is a cheat, but together, ginger, garlic, and scallions make the holy trinity of Chinese cooking. Cooked, raw, or somewhere in between (say sizzled with a pour of hot oil), they offer an incredible breadth of flavor and texture, alone or together.

SERVES 6

best mashed potatoes

@cookingwithshereen

If you've ever wondered what makes restaurant mashed potatoes taste so freaking good: It's butter. A special-occasion amount of butter. But sometimes you just need a decadent mound of carbs on your plate in the middle of the week, and only the best mashed potatoes will do. Chef Shereen says that getting a light, whipped texture in your mashed potatoes is the sign of a great chef (and home cook). Let her hold your hand through the process.

3 pounds / 1.4kg russet or Yukon Gold potatoes, peeled and cut into 1-inch / 2.5cm pieces

Salt (Shereen uses kosher)

1½ sticks (6 ounces / 170g) unsalted butter, at room temperature (#lifehack, page 148), plus more for serving

½ cup / 120ml heavy cream or double cream

Thinly sliced chives, for serving

Put the potatoes into a large pot and cover with cold water. Season generously with salt and bring to a boil over high heat.

Cook until tender, 10 to 12 minutes. Drain the potatoes and immediately return them to the pot. Let sit for 5 minutes, uncovered, off the heat. The residual heat of the pot will evaporate the excess moisture in the potatoes. (Don't skip this step! If you do, the end result will be watery.)

Meanwhile, in a small pot, melt the butter over medium-low heat, while constantly swirling the pot slowly. Add the cream and heat while stirring, until warmed through, 1 to 2 minutes. Do not let the cream bubble. Remove from the heat.

Working in batches, put the potatoes into a ricer or a food mill, pressing them through into a large bowl. When you've riced all the potatoes, pour the warmed butter mixture into the bowl and stir until the cream and butter are absorbed into the potatoes. They should be whipped, thick, and silky smooth—no lumps! Season with salt, then taste and add more salt if necessary.

Transfer to a serving bowl and add a couple pats of butter to melt over the top, and garnish with chives, because you're fancy. Serve immediately.

If the plantains are too hard to smash after the first fry, cook them a little longer and try again!

**UNDER
30 MINUTES**

SERVES 4

VEGAN

perfect tostones

@cheflorena

Crispy and salty on the outside, tender on the inside, these green plantains are fried excellence. You can thank Lorena, who is a chef from Venezuela, for showing us her perfect way to make them. Her tostones might look a little different than what you're used to since she leaves the servings big—and impressive—by smashing them pretty thin.

In a large bowl, whisk together the salt, lemon juice, garlic, and 2 cups / 480ml water until the salt is dissolved.

Pour 2 inches / 5cm oil into a deep heavy-bottomed pan with a thermometer. Heat the oil to 300°F / 150°C. Line a plate with paper towels.

When the oil is ready, add the plantains and cook until they are light golden brown and cooked through so they'll smash easily, about 3 minutes. (Insert a sharp knife into the plantains to test them.) Use a slotted spoon to remove them and transfer to the paper towels to drain. Now heat the oil up to 350°F / 175°C.

Submerge the plantains in the seasoned water for 20 seconds. Remove and pat dry with paper towels. Using a plantain press or the back of a flat plate, smash the plantains until they are ¼ inch / 6mm thick and 4 to 5 inches / 10 to 13cm across.

Return the smashed plantains to the hot oil and fry them until golden brown, another 4 to 5 minutes. Use a slotted spoon to transfer the fried plantains to the paper towels to drain. Sprinkle with salt while hot, then serve.

FYI
For newbies, here's how to peel plantains: Cut the ends off, then cut three shallow slits down the length of the plantain—deep enough to cut through the peel but not the fruit. Remove each section of peel and discard. Work quickly so the plantain doesn't oxidize.

2 tablespoons Morton kosher salt (see page 13 for more on salt), plus more for serving

Juice of 1 lemon

2 garlic cloves, minced (#lifehack, page 22)

Neutral vegetable oil, for frying

2 green plantains, peeled and cut into slices 2 inches / 5cm thick (FYI, below)

Strawberry
Cream Puffs
(page 150)

sweet
treats

SERVES 2

3 large egg whites

2 tablespoons sugar

2 teaspoons cornstarch

1 teaspoon vanilla extract

Food coloring (optional)

cloud bread

@myhealthydish

Was this the trend that started the fluffy food craze? Perhaps—since whipped coffee (page 164) and cloud eggs (see page 25) are also a thing. My's version of cloud bread makes some smart adjustments, like adding vanilla extract to put it firmly into the "dessert" category and using only the amount of cornstarch necessary to bind everything together. Once you whip up your egg whites, you're just 30 minutes away from a satisfying squish, rip, and cotton candy–like bite.

Preheat the oven to 300°F / 150°C. Line a sheet pan with parchment paper.

In a stand mixer with the whisk (or a large bowl if using a handheld mixer), beat the egg whites on high speed until fluffy and stiff peaks form, about 3 minutes.

Add the sugar, cornstarch, vanilla, and 4 to 5 drops of food coloring (if using), or more until the color is as deep as you like. Then, using a rubber spatula, gently fold the ingredients to combine so the beaten whites don't deflate too much. Using the mixer again, beat the mixture on high speed until incorporated, just a few seconds.

Turn the batter out onto the prepared pan and use the spatula or damp fingers to shape it into a loaf that's about 3 inches / 7.5cm tall (the other dimensions don't really matter).

Bake until the crust is light brown, about 25 mInutes. Cool for 5 minutes, then serve right away.

did you say . . . cloud bread?

Try with peppermint extract for minty clouds (tint: green) or lemon extract for citrusy ones (tint: yellow)!

for the best texture, pull them from the oven while still soft.

Add flaky salt after baking if that's your thing!

**MAKES
12 COOKIES**

peanut butter chocolate chip cookies

@chelsweets

Pro baker Chelsey puts her own spin on the super simple (gluten-free!) dough by adding big chunks of chocolate and a sprinkle of fancy salt on top. For the dough, save your "natural" peanut butter for another time and use something that doesn't need to be stirred in the jar for the right texture. These cookies bake quickly—trust that while they may not *look* very done after 10 minutes, they firm up as they cool. The hard part is waiting.

- **1 cup / 200g** (packed) light or dark brown sugar
- **1 large** egg, at room temperature
- **1 cup / 240g** smooth peanut butter (not "natural" peanut butter)
- **½ cup / 90g** chopped milk or dark chocolate chunks, plus **¼ cup / 45g** for topping (optional)
- **1 teaspoon / 6g** baking soda
- **½ teaspoon** coarse sea salt, for topping (optional)

Preheat the oven to 350°F / 175°C. Line a sheet pan with parchment paper or a silicone baking mat.

In a stand mixer with the paddle (or in a large bowl if using a handheld mixer), cream together the brown sugar and egg at medium speed until well combined, about 1 minute. If you don't have an electric mixer, give the mixture a good whisk by hand.

Add the peanut butter, chocolate, and baking soda and mix on a low speed until the cookie dough is smooth and no clumps of peanut butter remain, about 1 minute.

Scoop or roll 12 cookie dough balls (about 1 heaping tablespoon each) and put them on the prepared pan.

Bake until the tops of the cookies are just set, lightly cracked, and dry to the touch, 10 to 12 minutes. The cookies won't be firm or even darken much, but don't worry, they set quite a bit as they cool.

Remove from the oven and gently press a few additional chocolate chunks on top of the cookies and/or sprinkle with sea salt (if using either). Let the cookies cool on the sheet pan for 5 minutes before carefully transferring to a wire rack to cool completely.

**MAKES
16 BROWNIES**

1 **cup / 200g** granulated sugar

1 **cup / 200g** (packed) dark brown sugar

2 **sticks (8 ounces / 225g)** unsalted butter, melted and cooled

3 **large** eggs

1 **tablespoon** brewed coffee, cooled slightly or cold (just not too hot)

2 **teaspoons** vanilla extract

1½ **cups / 210g** all-purpose flour (#lifehack, page 155)

1 **cup / 80g** unsweetened cocoa powder

1½ **teaspoons** table salt (see page 13 for more on salt)

fudgy brownies

@thesweetimpact

Robert is a self-taught baker who's also a jaw-dropping cake artist. If you aren't already familiar with the very specific type of ASMR that is cake decorating videos, you need to follow him immediately. His page *also* features home baker–friendly desserts if you don't have quite the proficiency with fondant that he does.

Preheat the oven to 350°F / 175°C. Mist a 9 × 13-inch / 24 × 36cm baking pan with cooking spray.

In a large bowl, mix the sugar and dark brown sugar together with a spatula until no lumps remain. Add the melted butter and mix until thoroughly combined. Add the eggs one at a time, mixing until each is incorporated before adding the next egg. Finally, add the coffee and vanilla and mix until combined.

In a medium bowl, sift together the flour, cocoa powder, and salt, then whisk them until no traces of flour are visible. Gradually add the dry ingredients into the wet ingredients, folding with the spatula until just combined. Pour the batter into the prepared pan and use the spatula to spread the batter into an even layer.

Bake until the top has started to crack and looks a little less glossy, 20 to 25 minutes.

Allow the brownies to completely cool in the pan on a wire rack before cutting and serving. Store any extras in an airtight container at room temperature for up to 4 days.

Secret ingredient: coffee! (shhh)

go for granny smith if you like it tart—or gala if you're into sweet!

SERVES 4

2 **medium** apples, peeled if you like, cored, and thinly sliced

½ **cup / 100g** dark brown sugar, not packed

6 **tablespoons (3 ounces / 85g)** unsalted butter, melted

1 **teaspoon** ground cinnamon, or to taste

¼ **teaspoon** ground allspice, or to taste

⅛ **teaspoon** ground ginger, or to taste (optional)

Salt

1 frozen puff pastry sheet, thawed

1 **large** egg

Confectioners' sugar (optional)

apple pie tarts

@theres.food.at.home

Next time you're at the grocery store, take a little detour deep into the freezer aisle to pick up some frozen puff pastry—you'll be 50 percent of the way done with this easier-than-it-has-a-right-to-be dessert. Restaurateur and all-around cooking boss August offers guidelines for spicing your apples, so you can add more of what you like and skip what you don't.

Preheat the oven to 400°F / 200°C. Line a sheet pan with parchment paper or mist with cooking spray.

In a large bowl, combine the apples, brown sugar, melted butter, cinnamon, allspice, ginger (if using), and a pinch of salt. Toss to coat the apples thoroughly. Taste and add more spices and salt, if desired.

Cut the puff pastry sheet into 4 equal rectangles. Place the pastry pieces on the prepared sheet pan.

Divide the apple mixture evenly among the rectangles, leaving a small border around the edges. It's okay if a few apple slices overlap. Brush 1 tablespoon of the sugar mix left in the bowl onto each of the tarts (you might be tempted to add more, but it could make the tarts too soggy).

In a small bowl, beat the egg with 2 tablespoons water. Brush some of the egg wash on the exposed edges of each of the tarts.

Bake until the edges are golden brown, 15 to 20 minutes. Dust with confectioners' sugar, if you like, and serve warm.

**MAKES
18 PIECES**

Sugar Syrup

3 cups / 600g sugar

1 tablespoon fresh lemon
juice (#lifehack,
page 155)

2 cinnamon sticks

Baklava Rolls

Softened unsalted butter
(#lifehack, page 148), for
the pan

1⅓ cups / 185g pistachios

¾ cup / 100g almonds

1 teaspoon ground
cinnamon

1 (1-pound / 500g)
package large phyllo
dough sheets, at room
temperature

**2¾ sticks (11 ounces /
300g)** unsalted butter,
melted, or **1¼ cups /
300g** ghee, melted

crispy baklava rolls

@tazxbakes

**To get the most shattering crunch in each bite of this pistachio-
and-almond-filled baklava, Taz has a few tips for you: Don't let
your dough dry out, don't go crazy with the butter, and make
sure your syrup is completely cooled before pouring it all over
the fresh-out-of-the-oven rolls.**

Make the sugar syrup: In a medium pot, combine the sugar and
2 cups plus 2 tablespoons / 500ml water and bring to a boil over
medium-high heat, stirring regularly to dissolve the sugar. Add
the lemon juice and cinnamon sticks, reduce the heat, and gently
simmer for 15 minutes. Carefully pour the syrup into a heatproof
jar and set aside to cool completely. (It needs to be completely
cool before you pour it on the hot baklava. Do NOT pour hot or
even warm syrup on it!)

Make the baklava rolls: Preheat the oven to 325°F / 165°C.
Grease a 9 × 11-inch / 24 × 28cm baking dish with butter.

In a food processor, blitz 1 cup / 140g of the pistachios, the
almonds, and cinnamon until the pieces are about the size of a
grain of rice. Set aside.

Blitz the remaining ⅓ cup / 45g pistachios until finely ground, but
stop grinding before they turn into nut butter. Set aside.

Unfold one sheet of phyllo dough onto a clean work surface with
a short side facing you (cover the remaining sheets with a damp
towel to prevent them from drying out). Gently brush the sheet
with a thin layer of melted butter. Cover with a second sheet and
brush with butter. Sprinkle 2 tablespoons of the nut mixture over
the entire surface.

Recipe continues

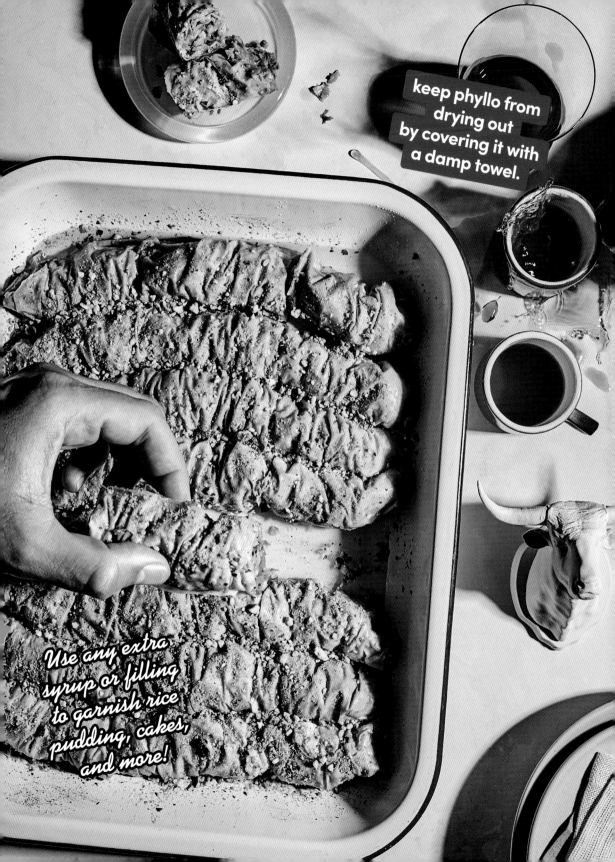

keep phyllo from
drying out
by covering it with
a damp towel.

*Use any extra
syrup or filling
to garnish rice
pudding, cakes,
and more!*

Place two wooden skewers end-to-end across the middle of the sheet horizontally and fold the sheet over (upward) in half to form a rectangle. The skewers should be inside the edge closest to you now. Carefully and loosely roll up the pastry rectangle around the skewers, starting from the edge closest to you. Push the ends of the roll down the skewers and toward the center to create a wrinkly roll that is 9 inches / 24cm long.

Lift the roll and carefully transfer to the prepared baking dish so it fits snugly along the shorter edge. Remove the skewers. Brush the roll with a thin layer of melted butter. Repeat with the remaining ingredients until you've filled the baking dish. (If you have leftover filling, you can store it in the freezer for up to 3 months and use it to garnish other desserts like rice pudding or cheesecake.)

Cut each roll into 3 pieces. Drizzle with the remaining butter.

Bake until the phyllo is golden brown and crisp, 45 to 60 minutes.

Remove from the oven and immediately pour over enough of the cooled syrup to cover the hot rolls. Allow them to soak for at least 1 hour. (The longer, the better—up to 24 hours!)

When you're ready to eat, drizzle with some of the remaining syrup, sprinkle with the ground pistachios, and serve.

Any extras can be covered and stored at room temperature for up to 2 weeks, or frozen for up to 3 months (thaw for at least 4 hours and up to overnight at room temperature).

#lifehack
If you don't have time to wait for butter or cream cheese to soften to room temperature, do this: Fill a tall drinking glass or glass bowl (large enough to fit your ingredient) with hot water, but not so hot as to shatter the glass. For butter: Stand the stick of butter upright on the counter, pour the hot water out of the glass, then invert the glass over the butter. For other ingredients: After pouring out the hot water, place the bowl over whatever you're softening. Check every few minutes until your dairy (or nondairy alternative) is just as soft as you need it.

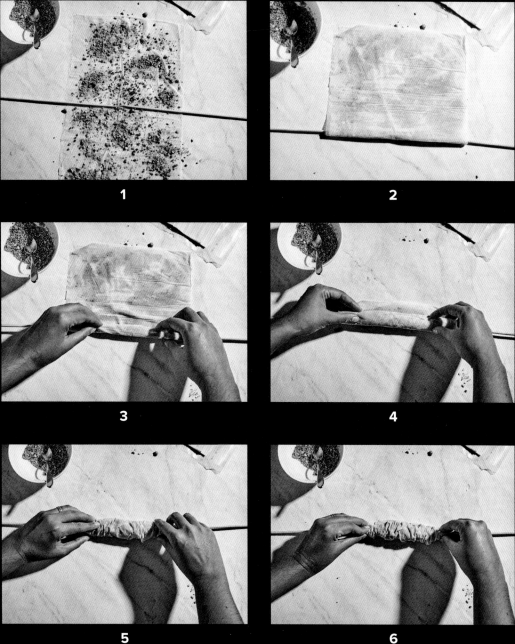

MAKES ABOUT
2 DOZEN
CREAM PUFFS

strawberry cream puffs

@scheckeats

Cream puffs get a rosy makeover from college cooking star Jeremy. He adds ground freeze-dried strawberries to whipped cream to create a bright, flavorful filling that certainly satisfies all the berries-and-cream fans out there. Jeremy's best advice? Read the whole recipe all the way through and visualize each step so you don't get confused or stuck in the middle.

Position a rack in the center of the oven and preheat the oven to 425°F / 220°C (or 400°F / 200°C for convection). Line 2 sheet pans with parchment paper or silicone baking mats.

Make the pâte à choux: In a medium saucepan, combine the milk, butter, sugar, salt, and ½ cup / 120ml water. Bring the mixture to a boil over low heat. Remove the pan from the heat immediately after it comes to a boil.

Pour in the flour all at once and mix with a wooden spoon until smooth. Return to medium heat and cook the dough, stirring constantly, for 2 minutes, until it looks like a thick paste and a light film forms on the bottom of the pan. Transfer the dough to a bowl and let it cool for 5 minutes.

Meanwhile, crack 4 eggs into a large measuring cup or small bowl. Beat them lightly with a fork.

After the dough has cooled for 5 minutes, add the beaten eggs in 4 additions, mixing vigorously with a wooden spoon after each addition until fully incorporated. (It may take a little elbow grease.) The finished dough should be slightly sticky and paste-like, but firm enough to hold after being piped. If yours looks too stiff, you may need to add the fifth egg. Beat the last egg in a small bowl and add half to the dough. Mix into the dough well and, if necessary, add the remaining beaten egg.

Pâte à Choux

½ cup / 120ml whole milk

1 stick (4 ounces / 115g) unsalted butter, cut into a few pieces

2 tablespoons sugar

½ teaspoon Diamond Crystal kosher salt (see page 13 for more on salt)

1 cup plus 1 tablespoon / 150g all-purpose flour (#lifehack, page 155)

5 large eggs, at room temperature

Strawberry Whipped Cream

1½ cups / 38g freeze-dried strawberries

¾ cup / 150g sugar

3 cups / 720ml heavy cream or double cream

4 fresh strawberries, hulled and thinly sliced

Let the dough cool slightly. (At this point you can store dough in an airtight container in the fridge for up to 2 days. You can also freeze the dough for up to 1 month and thaw it in the fridge overnight whenever you need it.)

Transfer the dough to a piping bag (see the #lifehack to the right) and use a 1M star tip. Fill a small bowl with water and put it by your work surface. Pipe onto the prepared pan in a circular motion as if you were frosting a cupcake, leaving room for each to puff up (you will need to bake in batches). Each glob of dough should be about 2 inches / 5cm wide. Dip your finger in water and gently press the point on the top down. (If you don't have a piping bag, you can use a small cookie dough scoop, or spoon ¼ cup / 60g of the dough onto the pan to form each cream puff.)

Put only one sheet pan in the oven and bake until browned and puffed, about 15 minutes, then reduce the temperature to 350°F / 175°C (or 325°F / 165°C for convection). If this happens in your oven after only 10 minutes, reduce the temperature sooner. Bake until the dough is puffed up and deep golden brown, another 15 to 20 minutes. Do not open the oven while baking.

Remove the pan from the oven and immediately use a paring knife to make a small slit in the bottom of each choux to let steam escape. Transfer to a wire rack to cool. Repeat with the remaining dough, but don't forget to increase the oven temperature first.

When they have cooled completely, cut each in half horizontally.

Meanwhile, make the strawberry whipped cream: In a blender or food processor, combine the freeze-dried strawberries and sugar and blend until they are a fine powder. In a large bowl, combine the heavy cream and strawberry powder. Use a handheld mixer on medium speed or a whisk and whip to stiff peaks. Transfer the whipped cream to a piping bag.

To serve, pipe as much cream as you'd like into the bottom half of the baked pâte à choux pastry (don't worry, there's plenty!) and top with a piece of fresh strawberry and the top half of the pastry.

Store any extras in an airtight container in the fridge for up to 2 days.

Bonus: Extra whipped cream can be used to top pancakes, dolloped on a slice of cake, or whipped more until it turns into strawberry butter.

#lifehack
The easiest, quickest way to prep your piping bag: First, measure your piping tip and cut half the length of the tip from the end of the bag (if your tip is 1 inch / 2.5cm long, cut ½ inch / 1.3cm from the closed end of the bag). Put the tip in the bag. Take a tall glass, place the bag with the tip down into the glass and fold the open end of the bag over the sides of the glass like a cuff. Now it will stay open for you to fill.

Chaheti uses cocettes, but any ovenproof dish that holds 8 ounces / 240ml or is about 3½ inches / 8.5cm wide and 2 inches / 5cm deep works.

The imperfect edges of the parchment help with that rustic wrinkled look.

SERVES 2

mini burnt basque cheesecakes

@rootedinspice

Inspired by a trip to the Basque Country where she fell for pastelitos—aka tiny cakes—and after tons of trial and error, Chaheti made the cutest and unfussiest mini cheesecake recipe you'll come across. You just blend, pour, bake. Because these are small, it's very important to keep an eye on them so they don't overcook.

In a small blender, combine the cream cheese, cream, sugar, flour, lemon zest, vanilla, egg, and a pinch of salt. Blend for 10 seconds, just to mix. Do not overblend! Let the mixture sit for 30 minutes to get rid of any air bubbles.

Position an oven rack about 6 inches / 15cm from the top and preheat the oven to 450°F / 230°C (or 425°F / 220°C for convection). Line two 8-ounce / 240ml cocottes or similar size ramekins with a square of parchment paper, with some coming up and over the sides of the dish. Press down and crease the paper in really well. Stir the batter a few times and pour into the prepared ramekins, leaving ½ inch / 1.3cm of space at the top of each.

Place the cocottes in the center of the top rack and bake for 20 minutes, then check. If the tops are browning nicely, bake until the tops are dark brown but the cheesecake still jiggles when shaken, up to another 5 minutes. If the tops aren't dark brown after 20 minutes, turn on the broiler to cook for just a few minutes, until nicely browned. Don't cook for longer than 30 minutes total or they'll be overcooked.

Transfer the cheesecakes to a rack to cool until the center sinks, then remove from the ramekins and put in the fridge for at least 2 hours, but ideally overnight (no need to cover). Serve chilled.

⅔ cup / 150g cream cheese, at room temperature (#lifehack, page 148)

⅓ cup / 80ml heavy cream or double cream

¼ cup / 50g sugar

1 tablespoon all-purpose flour

½ teaspoon grated lemon zest

⅛ teaspoon vanilla extract

1 large egg, at room temperature

Salt

**SERVES
8 TO 10**

VEGAN

rose-matcha olive oil cake

@lahbco

Presenting: a casually vegan cake to serve with a scoop of ice cream (dairy or nondairy). Nasim, a mostly plant-based cook, was inspired by floral Persian love cakes and a passion for matcha to make this sophisticated cake for a bestie. Olive oil cakes are great for every level of baker, thanks to a super-forgiving batter that bakes up beautifully and stores well for days.

Make the cake: Position a rack in the center of the oven and preheat the oven to 350°F / 175°C. Grease a 9-inch / 23cm round cake pan with olive oil and line the bottom with a round of parchment paper.

In a small bowl, mix the ground flaxseeds and 6 tablespoons water. Let the mixture sit until gelatinous, 10 to 15 minutes.

In a medium bowl, whisk together the flour, matcha, baking powder, and salt until combined.

In a large bowl, whisk together the sugar and olive oil until incorporated. Add the flax mixture, milk, and rose water. Whisk until combined.

Add the dry ingredients to the wet ingredients and use a spatula to fold until just barely combined. Be sure to not overmix the batter or your cake will be too dense. Pour the batter into the prepared pan and lightly tap the bottom of the pan on a hard surface to remove any air bubbles.

Bake until a toothpick inserted into the center comes out clean, 30 to 40 minutes. Let the cake cool completely in the pan, then remove it to a rack.

Cake

Olive oil, for the pan

2 tablespoons ground flaxseeds

1½ cups / 210g all-purpose flour (#lifehack, opposite)

2 tablespoons matcha powder, sifted, plus more for garnish

1 teaspoon baking powder

½ teaspoon Morton kosher salt (see page 13 for more on salt)

1 cup / 200g granulated sugar

¾ cup / 180ml extra-virgin olive oil

¼ cup / 60ml any unsweetened nondairy milk

1 tablespoon plus 1½ teaspoons rose water

While the cake cools, make the rose glaze: Sift the confectioners' sugar into a medium bowl. Add the rose water, lemon juice, and a sprinkle of salt and whisk until completely smooth.

Once the cake is cooled, poke a couple of holes on the surface with a fork. Slowly pour the glaze over the top of the cake. Garnish with a dusting of matcha and rose petals, and serve.

The cake can be stored in an airtight container at room temperature for up to 4 days and in the fridge for up to 1 week.

#lifehack
Another way to measure ingredients by weight is the "reverse tare." Instead of pouring your ingredients into a mixing bowl and adding the weight *up*, tare your scale with the container (of flour, or whatever) on it and measure *down* as you scoop out what you need into the mixing bowl. This is especially good when you're adding ingredients to a running mixer or a bubbling pot.

#lifehack
If you just need a little bit of lemon juice, but don't want to cut into a whole new lemon (or squeeze a lemon half into a tiny measuring spoon), try this: Use a skewer to poke one of the ends of a lemon, making sure you pierce all the way through the rind. Squeeze the lemon and the juice will come right out!

Rose Glaze

1 cup / 120g confectioners' sugar

2 tablespoons rose water

1 tablespoon fresh lemon juice (#lifehack, below)

Salt

Fresh or dried rose petals, for serving

**MAKES ONE
6-INCH / 15CM
CAKE**

level-up layer cake

@colinstimetobake

This triple-layer cake from Scottish baking whiz Colin lets you flex as hard as you like. The cakes will come out perfectly light and fluffy thanks to a little help from cornstarch, which doesn't weigh the batter down as much as flour. Colin gives you a few ways to frost the cake. Are you a pro with a piping bag? Make rosettes. Not as comfortable? Slather on the frosting with a table knife and serve it up. Whoever's eating it will still be very impressed.

Make the cake: Position an oven rack in the center of the oven and preheat the oven to 300°F / 150°C. Lightly butter three 6-inch / 15cm cake pans, then line the bottoms with rounds of parchment paper. (If you just have one or two pans, you can work in batches.) Lightly butter the parchment paper.

In a stand mixer with the whisk (or a large bowl if using a handheld mixer), beat the butter on medium speed until smooth and creamy, about 2 minutes. Add the sugar into the bowl. Beat on medium until the mixture is thick and the color has lightened, 2 to 3 minutes. Scrape down the sides.

Add 1 egg and beat on medium until completely combined, about 1 minute. Scrape down the sides of the bowl. Repeat with the remaining eggs, adding them one at a time. Your mixture should be glossy. If it looks slightly curdled, beat it a few seconds more, until emulsified.

In a medium bowl, stir together the flour, cornstarch, and baking powder. In a small cup or bowl, mix together the milk and vanilla.

Recipe continues

Cake

Softened butter (#lifehack, page 148), for the pans

2 sticks (8 ounces / 225g) unsalted butter, at room temperature

1½ cups / 300g superfine sugar

4 large eggs, at room temperature

2 cups / 280g all-purpose flour (#lifehack, page 155)

2 tablespoons cornstarch

2 teaspoons baking powder

6 tablespoons whole milk

2 teaspoons vanilla extract

Frosting and Filling

4 sticks (1 pound / 455g) unsalted butter, at room temperature

7½ cups / 900g confectioners' sugar

1 tablespoon vanilla extract

Food coloring of your choice (optional)

½ cup / 150g raspberry jam

A few pastry tips and a pastry bag make creating scalloped edges and rosettes a breeze.

Turn the mixer to medium and add one-third of the flour mixture, mixing just until the flour is incorporated. Stop and scrape down the sides of the bowl. Add half the milk mixture and beat on medium until just combined, then scrape down the sides. Add the remaining flour mixture in two additions alternating with the remaining milk mixture, scraping down the sides after each addition. The batter should be the texture of a thick mousse.

Divide the batter evenly among the three prepared cake pans, spreading it in an even layer. If you're working in batches, cover the remaining batter with plastic wrap and refrigerate until needed or up to 24 hours.

Bake the cakes for 40 minutes, then check. The cake will be done when there is a slight wobble in the middle and a knife or cake tester inserted into the center of the cake comes out clean. If the cakes are not ready at 40 minutes, bake in 10-minute intervals until done.

Cool the cakes in the pans for 10 minutes. Run a knife or offset spatula around the cakes to loosen them. Place a wire rack on top of one of the pans. Use a towel to protect your hands and invert the pan and rack together. Remove the pan, peel off the parchment paper, and let the cake cool completely. Repeat with the other cakes. If any of the cakes has a domed top, use a serrated knife to level off the top once completely cool.

While the cakes cool, make the frosting: In a stand mixer with the whisk (or a large bowl if using a handheld mixer), beat the butter on medium speed until smooth, about 2 minutes. With the machine still running, add the confectioners' sugar gradually until fully incorporated. Blend in the vanilla. Finally add the food coloring (if using) a drop at a time, until the frosting is your desired shade.

To assemble the cake, place one cake layer onto a serving plate. Using an offset spatula or the rounded end of a dessert spoon, gently spread an even ½ inch / 1.3cm layer of frosting on top, leaving a ½-inch / 1.3cm border around the edges (you don't want it to leak out). Spread half the raspberry jam over the frosting. Place another cake layer on top and repeat. Top with the final cake layer.

Using an offset spatula or the rounded end of a dessert spoon, smooth a thin layer of frosting onto the side and top of the cake. Put in the fridge for 20 minutes to set. (This is called a "crumb coat.")

Spread a thick layer of frosting on the top and side with an offset spatula or butter knife, completely covering the cake. You can leave it like this, or smooth it down with a scraper.

Slice and serve the cake, or store in an airtight container in a cool, dry place for up to 3 days.

FYI
Level up with some very professional-looking roses made with frosting:

Cover with the crumb coat as directed. Put a 1M piping tip into a pastry bag and fill the bag halfway with room-temperature frosting (#lifehack, page 151).

Position your piping bag perpendicular to the cake, starting from where the center of the rosette will be. Begin piping, moving in a clockwise motion, and spiraling out and around your center spot, moving outward until you have a flower that's 1½ inches / 4cm in diameter. (You can make a test rosette on parchment paper first, if you like.)

Start piping rosettes from the base of the cake and work your way up the side, completely covering the cake. Move to the top of the cake and pipe around the edge first. Finish with a large rosette in the center.

Make into a kulfi sandwich by spreading some between two of your fave cookies!

SERVES 6

14 Oreo cookies, plus more (optional) for serving

1 cup / 240ml whole milk

½ cup / 120ml heavy cream or double cream

⅓ cup / 65g sugar

5 tablespoons sweetened condensed milk

¼ cup / 35g milk powder (whole or nonfat; both work)

1 teaspoon fine sea salt (see page 13 for more on salt)

cookies and cream kulfi

@goldengully

This no-churn (aka chill) dessert was inspired by Bilal's followers. When he got tons of requests for an Oreo version . . . well, you know what happened. The not-so-secret ingredients are sweetened condensed milk (which gives it the uniquely kulfi flavor), the milk powder (which provides the satisfying chew you won't be able to get enough of), and a good amount of salt for a nicely balanced bite.

In a food processor or blender, process the cookies until they turn into fine crumbs (it's okay if there are a few larger pieces of creme, but make sure the wafer parts of the cookies are all broken up). Measure out 1 cup / 160g of crumbs and save any extra for sundaes.

In the food processor or blender, combine the crumbs, whole milk, cream, sugar, condensed milk, milk powder, and salt. Blend until smooth.

Pour the mixture into ice pop molds or a freezer-safe container (like a bowl) and freeze until solid, at least 8 hours.

To serve, unmold the ice pops, or spoon the kulfi into bowls, or make a kulfi sandwich by splitting an Oreo and spreading the kulfi between the two wafers.

Large-Batch
Bourbon, Peach,
and Ginger
Arnold Palmer
(page 177)

day and night beverages

**UNDER
30 MINUTES**

SERVES 1

2 tablespoons sugar

2 tablespoons plain
instant coffee crystals

2 to 3 tablespoons
caramel sauce, to taste

Ice, if using cold milk

½ cup / 120ml any milk,
or more if you like, hot
or cold

dalgona coffee
with caramel

@cookingwithlynja

**Named for the South Korean sweet it resembles, Dalgona
coffee had a moment . . . and is still having that moment. It's
easy. It's fancy. And it's slightly mysterious. How do coffee,
sugar, and water turn into a nice, thick foam in a "Timberland
boots brown" (Lynja's words)? Check out page 167 for the
answer, then make Lynja's take on the trend that goes heavy on
the caramel.**

In a medium bowl, stir together the sugar, coffee crystals, and
2 tablespoons cold water.

If using a hand mixer, mix on medium-high speed until light brown
in color and doubled in volume, 2 to 4 minutes. If whisking by
hand, 8 to 10 minutes.

Drizzle the caramel sauce around the inside of a glass or mug. If
making a cold drink, fill the glass with ice. Pour the milk into the
glass and then spoon the coffee cream on top of the milk. Serve
immediately.

if doubling or tripling the recipe, use a stand mixer.

Iced "Dalgona" Matcha Latte (page 166)

**UNDER
30 MINUTES**

SERVES 1

¼ cup / 60ml heavy cream
or double cream

1 to 2 tablespoons sugar,
to taste

1 to 2 teaspoons matcha
powder, to taste

Ice, for serving

1 cup / 240ml any vanilla-
flavored almond milk or
other nondairy milk

iced "dalgona"
matcha latte

@beautifuleatsandthings

Yes, instant coffee is the key ingredient in a Dalgona latte, but that doesn't mean matcha fans should be left out of the trend. Andrea, the body-positive dietitian and contender for "happiest follow," has the perfect spin. She swapped out the water in the foam for cream, since matcha doesn't have the same magic-foaming compound coffee does, so you still get that thick texture.

In a medium bowl, stir together the cream, sugar, and matcha.

If using a handheld mixer, mix on medium-high speed until smooth, creamy, and thick, 1 to 2 minutes. If whisking by hand, whisk until stiff peaks form, 2 to 3 minutes. (There's a trade-off here: If you use a mixer, it will be easier, but if you whisk by hand you can get nice, stiff foam. Up to you!)

Fill your serving glass with ice. Pour in the almond milk and top with the whipped matcha. Stir together or leave the foam on top for an impressive presentation and serve right away.

the dalgona download

Make no mistake: This isn't about troubleshooting. If you follow @cookingwithlynja's recipe on page 164, your coffee will stick the landing every time. But with only four ingredients (muscle power counts as one), it's good to know the hows and whys if you're thinking about experimenting or want to find out why you had some Dalgona heartbreak in the past.

There's Only One Right Coffee

You must use plain instant coffee, not the three-in-one kind or any flavored variety. That's because instant coffee has a high concentration of compounds called surfactants, an abbreviation for "surface active agents," which hold gas and liquid together. They're how you can turn instant coffee, water, and sugar into coffee magic! They're found naturally in coffee and it's what causes that dreamy crema on a shot of espresso.

Sugar Is Required

You *can* whip up instant coffee without the sugar, but the foam will almost immediately start to deflate. If you want your foam to be dense and smooth (and stick around long enough to get a few good pictures in), you have to use a decent amount of sugar. For many recipes, it's 1:1 coffee to sugar.

Cold Water, Please

Whether you're making an iced latte or a hot one, use cold water to dissolve the coffee. Hot water will bring out more bitter flavors from the instant coffee—think about the flavor difference between hot coffee and cold brew—which doesn't make for a pleasant whipped coffee experience.

Whip It Up

You've got options here, depending on how much work you want to put in. A handheld mixer is your best bet because it's the perfect compromise between a stand mixer (too big to produce thick foam) and a whisk (sore arms), but all three work. Some people swear by the mason jar method of shaking, but if you're going to use all that upper body strength, you're better off whisking. The foam will be so much thicker.

for the smoothest and richest milk tea, the guys recommend loose leaf tea.

SERVES 4

hong kong milk tea with slanted coffee jelly

@bobaguys

Coffee jelly—coffee and sugar set with gelatin—is all over Japan, where Andrew and Bin drew their inspiration. And in many places in Asia a half-coffee, half-tea combo (known as yinyong) is a signature beverage. When they brought coffee-tea back to California, they put their own spin on it for two reasons: The A+ aesthetics of the set jelly and reclaiming the idea that "slanted is beautiful." Not only was it an immediate hit, it was a cultural commentary to address anti-Asian hate.

Make the coffee jelly: Pour ½ cup / 120ml cold water into a small bowl. Sprinkle the gelatin over the top and let the mixture sit, undisturbed, for 10 minutes.

Meanwhile, in a small saucepan, bring the coffee to a simmer over medium-low heat. Add the brown sugar and stir until fully dissolved, then return to a simmer. Remove from the heat and add the gelatin mixture. (If your gelatin is very solid at this point, add a little bit of the hot coffee into the small bowl to loosen it first.) Mix until everything dissolves and there are no visible gelatin clumps. Cool to room temperature but do not put it in the fridge yet!

Once the coffee jelly is cooled, distribute the mixture among four 16-ounce / 475ml glasses. Put a muffin tin (or small ramekins if you don't have a muffin tin) in the fridge. Put the glasses into the muffin tin cups and tilt each glass a bit, so the jelly will set slanted. (The muffin tin will help hold the glasses in place, and you can also put a ball of aluminum foil under each glass to keep it at a tilt.) Refrigerate for at least 4 hours or up to overnight to set.

Recipe continues

Coffee Jelly

- **4 teaspoons** powdered gelatin
- **2 cups / 480ml** coffee or cold brew, any temperature
- **6 tablespoons / 75g** (packed) light brown sugar

Milk Tea

- **2 cups / 275g** ice, plus more for serving
- **½ cup / 40g** loose black tea leaves or 8 tea bags (FYI, page 170)
- **½ cup plus 2 tablespoons / 200g** sweetened condensed milk

Make the milk tea: Put the ice in a medium bowl. In a small saucepan, bring 3 cups / 720ml water to a simmer over high heat. Remove from the heat and add the tea. Steep the tea for 4 minutes, then strain over the ice. While the ice is melting, mix in the condensed milk. Stir until everything is fully incorporated. Put in the fridge to chill (ideally while the coffee jelly solidifies).

When the coffee jelly has set, remove the glasses from the fridge. Add a handful of ice to each glass. Slowly pour 1 cup / 240ml of the milk tea over the ice in each glass. Serve with a spoon and a straw.

FYI
The Boba Guys use loose-leaf tea, and specifically a small-leaf tea blend of Assam, Ceylon, and Yunnan leaves. If the tea leaves you've got at home are large and wispy—so there's less in your measurement—steep the tea for another 1 to 2 minutes to make sure it's strong enough to stand up to the milk.

**UNDER
30 MINUTES**

**SERVES
2 OR 3**

1 **tablespoon** grated
   peeled fresh ginger

1 **teaspoon** ajwain seeds

1 **teaspoon** fennel seeds

6 cardamom pods

4 whole cloves

¼ **to** ½ cinnamon stick

2 **to 3 tablespoons** loose
   black tea leaves
   or 2 or 3 black tea bags,
   to taste

2 **cups / 480ml** whole
   or part skim milk or
   unsweetened oat milk

Sugar, for serving

masala chai

@goldengully

**Let Bilal lead you to your just-right version of masala chai.
There really aren't any hard-and-fast measurements for his
favorite drink, so think of this as an outline and start by making
the recipe as directed to get a sense of what you do and don't
like. Then, start riffing. Add more ginger if you love the heat,
reduce the tea if you like a milder brew. Try it with oat milk
just for fun. The perfect masala chai is however you choose to
make it.**

In a small pot (at least 1 quart / 1 liter), heat 2 cups / 480ml water
over high heat. When small bubbles begin to form, add the ginger,
ajwain seeds, fennel seeds, cardamom, cloves, and cinnamon.
Cook for 2 minutes, adjusting the heat, if necessary, to keep the
mixture from boiling.

Add the tea and bring the mixture to a boil. Boil for 2 minutes,
then add the milk. Let the mixture come back to a boil, and when
the mixture bubbles up and almost reaches the top of the pot,
quickly reduce the heat to medium-low (don't walk away—this
happens fast). Simmer for 5 minutes. Taste, and if you like your
chai stronger, repeat the bubbling up and 5-minute simmer
process.

Spoon sugar to taste into serving cups, then pour the chai
through a fine-mesh sieve into the cups. Stir to dissolve the sugar
and serve right away.

UNDER 30 MINUTES **SERVES 1** **VEGAN**

1 ounce / 30ml fresh lime juice

½ ounce / 15ml simple syrup

4 (1-inch / 2.5cm) watermelon cubes

1½ ounces / 45ml cachaça

¾ ounce / 25ml mezcal

Ice, for serving

1 sprig fresh rosemary

the brazilian mariachi

@thelucasassis_

Cocktail genius Lucas came up with this instant-classic of a bev for his wedding. He combined his native Brazil's national spirit, cachaça, with mezcal to rep his wife's Mexican heritage and added some watermelon to make a drink you'll want to sip (if you're 21+) all summer long.

In a cocktail shaker, combine the lime juice, simple syrup, and watermelon. Use a muddler to muddle for 10 seconds. Add the cachaça and mezcal and fill the shaker with ice. Cover the shaker securely and shake vigorously for 10 to 15 seconds.

Fill a rocks glass with ice and using a double-strainer or fine-mesh sieve, strain the cocktail into the glass.

Using a kitchen blowtorch or lighter, singe the rosemary just until aromatic. Garnish the glass with the rosemary and serve.

FYI
Want to make a cocktail for all your friends but don't want to shake each individually? Batch it up! In a large pitcher, combine ⅓ cup / 80ml simple syrup, ½ cup / 120ml mezcal, ⅔ cup / 160ml fresh lime juice, 1 cup / 240ml cachaça, 1¼ cups / 300ml watermelon juice (or 22 cubes of watermelon, muddled), and ¼ cup / 60ml water (the water is important and necessary to help create the dilution usually caused by shaking with ice). Stir it all together and pour into ice-filled glasses.

SERVES 8

VEGAN

Mulling Spices Syrup

1 cup / 200g sugar

¼ cup / 30g mulling spices

Punch

1½ cups / 355ml Plantation Pineapple Rum

1¼ cups / 295ml fresh tart apple cider

⅔ cup / 150ml fresh lemon juice

12 dashes orange bitters

8 cups / 1.2kg ice, for serving

1 apple, cored and thinly sliced

cider rum punch

@spiritedla

Queen of #drink TikTok Hannah played up cider's sweet-tart perfection with pineapple rum, a spiced-infused syrup, and fresh lemon juice for a perfect cool-weather drink. If you're having trouble finding pineapple rum, Hannah says to go ahead and swap in an aged rum and your fellow drinkers will be just as happy. Pro tip: There will be extra syrup—try it in an old fashioned!

Make the mulling spices syrup: In a medium saucepan, bring 1 cup / 240ml water to a boil, then add the sugar and stir until it dissolves. Add the mulling spices and simmer for 10 minutes, stirring occasionally. Remove from the heat and allow it to cool completely.

Strain the cooled syrup through a fine-mesh sieve and discard the solids. Store the syrup in a tightly sealed container in the fridge for up to 1 week.

Make the punch: In a large pitcher or punch bowl, combine the rum and cider. Strain the lemon juice through a fine-mesh sieve to remove any pulp, then add to the pitcher or bowl. Pour in ⅔ cup / 150ml of the mulling spices syrup and add the orange bitters. Taste and add up to ¼ cup / 60ml more syrup if you like your cocktail sweeter.

Add the ice to the pitcher or punch bowl (enough to fill it), then stir 50 times (Hannah says this amount gets you the optimal temperature and dilution). Add the apple slices and ladle into serving glasses.

UNDER 30 MINUTES

SERVES 1

1 grapefruit wedge, 1½ inches / 1.3m wide

Sugar (optional)

1 lime wedge

Sal de gusano or Tajín

Ice, for serving

1½ ounces / 45ml fresh grapefruit juice

¾ ounce / 25ml fresh lime juice

½ ounce / 15ml simple syrup

1 ounce / 30ml tequila blanco

1 ounce / 30ml mezcal

Topo Chico sparkling water, for topping

my classic paloma

@thelucasassis_

Contrary to popular belief, the national cocktail of Mexico is not the margarita—it's the paloma! Lucas put his skillful bartender twist on the cocktail and made some upgrades you're going to flip out for. He uses sal de gusano for the rim—a Oaxacan salt mixture featuring toasted and ground larvae called chinicuil, which give it an earthy, umami kick. He garnishes the cocktail with a made-to-order brûléed grapefruit and finishes the drink with sparkling water.

To make a caramelized grapefruit garnish (which is optional), sprinkle the grapefruit wedge with a thin, even layer of sugar. Using a kitchen blowtorch, heat the sugar, just until bubbling and golden. Let cool while you make the cocktail.

Run the lime wedge around the rim of a collins glass. Pour a thin layer of sal de gusano on a small plate, then dip the rim of the glass in the salt to coat. Fill the glass with ice.

To the glass, add the grapefruit juice, lime juice, simple syrup, tequila, and mezcal. Stir with a bar spoon. Top with sparkling water, garnish with the caramelized or plain grapefruit wedge, and serve.

FYI
If you want to make cocktails for you and five friends, in a large pitcher combine: 1¼ cups / 300ml of fresh grapefruit juice, ⅔ cup / 160ml of fresh lime juice, ⅓ cup / 80ml of simple syrup, ¾ cup / 180ml of tequila, and ¾ cup / 180ml of mezcal and stir. Garnish six collins glasses as directed, then fill with ice, and pour in the cocktail, leaving about three fingers of space in each. Top with Topo Chico.

"it has to be fresh!"

UNDER 30 MINUTES **SERVES 6** **VEGAN**

- **1½ cups / 355ml** unsweetened cold black tea

- **1 cup plus 2 tablespoons / 265ml** high-proof bourbon, such as Wild Turkey 101

- **½ cup plus 1 tablespoon / 135ml** peach liqueur

- **6 tablespoons / 90ml** ginger liqueur

- **⅔ cup / 150ml** fresh lemon juice

- **8 cups / 1.2kg** ice, for serving

- **2** medium peaches, thinly sliced

large-batch bourbon, peach, and ginger arnold palmer

@spiritedla

If you thought the Arnold Palmer was a great drink before, get ready for this glow-up. Hannah swapped out the lemonade for fresh lemon juice and two kinds of extra-refreshing sweet liqueurs. As she says, don't be afraid to up the amounts of the sweet stuff if that's how you like your cocktails. All you need is a pitcher or a punch bowl big enough, and a summer afternoon with nothing to do but hang.

In a large pitcher or punch bowl, combine the tea, bourbon, peach liqueur, and ginger liqueur. Strain the lemon juice through a fine-mesh sieve to remove any pulp, then add to the pitcher or punch bowl.

Add the ice to the pitcher or punch bowl (enough to fill it), then stir 50 times (Hannah says this amount gets you the optimal temperature and dilution). Add the peaches and ladle into serving glasses.

TikTok Is a Proud Supporter of
No Kid Hungry

 We want to inspire and encourage a new generation to have a positive impact on the planet and those around them, and as a company we are getting behind organizations we know are making a difference.

Every kid needs three meals a day to grow up healthy, happy, and strong. But today in America, too many children are missing those meals. This is a problem No Kid Hungry knows how to solve and we want to help make that possible. Together, we can help make no kid hungry in America a reality!

Scan the QR code to check out No Kid Hungry's TikTok account and learn more, or visit www.NoKidHungry.com.

acknowledgments

Thank you to all the home cooks, professional chefs, hobbyists, backyard barbecuers, air fryer fanatics, cake masters, pasta pros, steak stans, and more who make the cooking side of TikTok a delicious place to be. And thank you to the entire TikTok community and all of the creators. You inspire us every. single. day.

This cookbook wouldn't have been possible without the incredible team at Clarkson Potter. Raquel Pelzel, Sahara Clement, and Bianca Cruz shaped this book into something creators can be proud to be a part of. Robert Diaz, Ian Dingman, Windy Dorresteyn, Jill Flaxman, Derek Gullino, Francis Lam, Pete Mathias, Chris Tanigawa, Kate Tyler, Aaron Wehner, and Joyce Wong helped us at every step of the book creation process. And project manager/writer Emily Stephenson brought everything together seamlessly. Thank you to the dream team!

So much gratitude to Lauren Volo for the incredible photos of the creators' recipes. Along with Monica Pierini, Maeve Sheridan, Tsering Dolma, Claire Pellegrino, and Christina Zhang, these dishes pop off the page and make mouths water.

To the exacting recipe testers—Scott Hocker, Rémy Robert, and Grace Rosanova—thank you for confirming what we all know: These creators understood the assignment.

And thank you, reader, for supporting the brilliant creator community on TikTok.

TikTok creator index

@amywilichowski
Amy Wilichowski is a Registered Dietitian, small business owner, and content creator based in Boston, Massachusetts. In her spare time, you can find her rollerblading, brunching, creating a new recipe, or exploring the city with friends.
Pesto Egg Toast 27

@auntieloren
Loren Montgomery, also known as Auntie Loren, was raised in Valdosta, Georgia, but now resides in McDonough, Georgia, and works as a caterer and restaurant owner. She's a disabled Army veteran who loves to cook, listen to music, and spend time with her three kids and husband.
Hot Crab and Spinach Dip with Garlicky Toasts 49
Biscuit Pot Pie 100

@ballehurns
Halle Burns is a food and lifestyle content creator who quickly rose to fame with her soothing vegan cooking videos. Her relaxed approach has inspired a generation to get creative in their kitchens.
Vegan Pretzel Bites 46
Sweet Chile-Smashed Sprouts 127

@beautifuleatsandthings
Andrea is an Alabama-based Registered Dietitian Nutritionist and the blogger behind *Beautiful Eats & Things* and *Little Eats & Things*. Andrea is also the author of *The Complete Book of Smoothies*. She believes in achieving optimal health by incorporating healthier eating habits into your lifestyle and making healthy eating fun! When she's not running after her two toddlers, she enjoys creating content to encourage self-love and promote body positivity.
Easy Spinach Chicken Alfredo Flatbread Pizzas 67
Iced "Dalgona" Matcha Latte 166

@bobaguys
Boba Guys bridge cultures with their globally inspired specialty drinks. They've been taking boba and tea to the next level since 2011. Their cookbook, *The Boba Book*, came out in 2020.
Hong Kong Milk Tea with Slanted Coffee Jelly 169

@chefchrischo
Born in Korea and "braised" in Philadelphia, Chris comes from a family of chefs and learned how to cook when he was young. His goal is to make easy, authentic, and fun recipes for everyone to cook at home.
Shrimp Fried Rice 87
Korean Corn Cheese 125

@cheflorena
Venezuelan-born Lorena Garcia is well known for her numerous accomplishments, including being a cookbook author, a television host, and a restaurateur. Her nonprofit, Big Chef, Little Chef, helps children and their families take control of their eating habits and, ultimately, their lives.
Perfect Tostones 135

@chefmingtsai
Ming Tsai is the James Beard Award–winning chef/owner of Blue Dragon in Boston, Massachusetts, and BABA at the Yellowstone Club in Big Sky, Montana. An Emmy Award-winning TV host, he is also the author of five cookbooks. Ming launched his new line of veggie-filled patties, MingsBings, in fall 2020. Ming supports many charities, including Family Reach, a nonprofit whose mission is to provide financial relief and support to families fighting cancer, of which he is currently the Chairman of the National Advisory Board. For more visit www.ming.com.
Ming Tsai's Favorite Kitchen Gear 15

Beef Short Rib Birria "Super Crunk Wrap," 119

@chelsweets
Chelsey White is the blogger and content creator behind Chelsweets, teaches baking classes at the Institute of Culinary Education in NYC, and is also a digital contributor to the Food Network. Her work has been featured by BuzzFeed, Instagram, Business Insider, Bloomberg, the *Wall Street Journal*, and *Cosmopolitan*.
Peanut Butter Chocolate Chip Cookies 141

@chucksflavortrain
Chuck Matto, known by most as Chuck's Flavor Train, is a fun-loving culinary conductor. He's a ball of energy who will wow you with his delicious dishes and impress you with his quick-witted and clever narrations.
Reverse-Seared Steak 114

@colinstimetobake
Colin started baking in 2014 to keep himself busy. Much to his excitement, he realized other people wanted to watch the process, and Colin's Time to Bake website was born. He sells baked goods in the Chicago area and hopes to open a Scottish bakery.
Level-Up Layer Cake 156

@cookingbomb
Vivian Aronson grew up in Sichuan, China, and moved to the United States in 2005. She now lives in Minneapolis with her husband and four kids. Vivian was one of the top thirty-six contestants competing in *MasterChef* season 10 in 2019.
One-Tomato Lazy Rice 88
Hand-Pulled Cabbage with Bacon 130

@cookingwithlynja
Lynja Davis is a grandmother of two, mother of four, wife, retired AT&T engineer, volunteer EMT, eight-time marathon runner, animal lover (especially dogs), world traveler, Spanish student, MIT BS, and Columbia MBA and MPH. Her motto is: "Don't be afraid to make mistakes! Mistakes make you more resilient and confident!"
Ramen Carbonara 77
Dalgona Coffee with Caramel 164

@cookingwithshereen
Shereen Pavlides is a professionally trained chef, recipe developer, and food stylist, and has presented live on QVC, where she created *Cooking with Shereen*. Shereen helps others cook and feel like rock stars in their own kitchens.
Grilled Jalapeño Corn Off the Cob 128
Best Mashed Potatoes 133

@diana_mengyan
Mengyan Yu was born in China and has been living in Switzerland since 2017. Cooking is her passion, and she's on her way to discovering more cooking adventures.
Pan-Fried Pork and Chive Dumplings 57
Steamed Garlic Prawns with Vermicelli Noodles 78

@feelgoodfoodie
Yumna Jawad is the founder and CEO of Feel Good Foodie—a website dedicated to healthy-ish recipes with feel-good ingredients. She loves to inspire her followers to cook at home and have fun in the kitchen.
Salt and Vinegar Pasta Chips 50
Baked Feta Pasta Soup 82

@giadadelaurentiis
Giada De Laurentiis is the Emmy Award-winning star of *Everyday Italian, Giada Entertains, Giada at Home, Giada in Italy, Giada's Holiday Handbook,* and *Next Food Network Star.* She is the author of nine *New York Times* bestselling books and is the creative force behind the lifestyle platform Giadzy. Giada attended the Cordon Bleu cooking school in Paris and worked at Wolfgang Puck's Spago restaurant before starting her own catering company, GDL Foods. Born in Rome, she grew up in Los Angeles, where she now lives with her daughter, Jade.
Giada and Jade's Breakfast Croissant Paninis 24

@goldengully
Born and raised in Toronto, Canada, Bilal began sharing his love for home cooking on TikTok given he had spare time in 2020. Outside of

cooking, he practices Canadian immigration law and enjoys training in mixed martial arts.
Cookies and Cream Kulfi 161
Masala Chai 171

@gordonramsayofficial

Gordon Ramsay is a world renown chef, restaurateur, TV presenter, and dad. He's also now a TikTok star with his biting commentary on food from around the internet.

@guarnaschelli

Alex Guarnaschelli is a judge on numerous Food Network shows, including *Chopped* and *Beat Bobby Flay*, the host of her digital series *Fix Me a Plate*, and one of three women Iron Chefs on *Iron Chef America*. The daughter of esteemed cookbook editor Maria Guarnaschelli, Alex grew up in Manhattan, immersed in food. She moved to Paris to work at Guy Savoy for four years before returning to cook at Daniel. She has been the executive chef at Butter Restaurant since 2003 and lives in New York City with her daughter, Ava.
Alex Guarnaschelli's Tips for Pro Home Cooking 71

@hwoo.lee

h woo lee (AYch-wOO) is a food content creator, event planner, and founder of his underground fine-dining supper club, Maru Los Angeles. His high-intensity, quick-clip cooking videos showcase his culinary skills and personality.
Beef Short Rib Birria "Super Crunk Wrap" 119

@jerryyguerabide

Jerry is a San Antonio, Texas–bred chef with a passion for cooking. Having worked his way up through the brigade system, he's now continuing his culinary venture with Mesa de Magdalena, a food truck based in San Antonio.
Lemon Blueberry Biscuits 36
Marinated Riblets with Guajillo Salsa 111

@lahbco

Nasim Lahbichi is a home chef, born and raised in Brooklyn, New York. Growing up in the diverse and multicultural neighborhoods of Brooklyn allowed him to appreciate the nuances and intersectionality of food and culture. He wants to empower others through his recipes for approachable and delicious food.
Berry-Cheesecake Baked Oats 39
Rose-Matcha Olive Oil Cake 154

@myhealthydish

My Nguyen, the creator of MyHealthyDish, is a social media influencer, chef, and author. She has millions of followers who tune in daily for her recipes and to be inspired to live a healthier lifestyle. My resides in the San Francisco Bay Area with her husband, twin daughters, and two pups.
Pancake Cereal 34
Cloud Bread 138

@newt

Newt is a social-media personality and self-taught chef with a passion for food and learning about culinary arts. He shares his recipes on TikTok, teaching people how to cook with his step-by-step videos. He really likes parsley.
Bang-Bang Shrimp 54

@nishcooks

Joshuah Nishi, aka NishCooks, is a self-taught chef, recipe developer, food blogger, and content creator. He's known for his cooking videos and infectious sense of humor. Originally from Stockton, California, Joshuah grew up in a single-parent house where he would put together the ingredients that he found in the kitchen, turning each experience into a lesson and an opportunity to develop his skills.
Char Siu Chicken Banh Mis 69

@onegreatvegan

Gabrielle Reyes, also known as One Great Vegan, is an award-winning singer, actress, plant-based chef, cookbook author, and TV host. Creating Caribbean-Latin fusion and true soul food was how Gabrielle grew up, eating inexpensive, flavor-packed meals that she now veganizes with tasty tunes and savory songs.
"Cheesy" Vegan Tortilla 53
Haitian Jackfruit Enchiladas 103

@ramenkingivan

Ivan McCombs, better known as the Ramen King, started making TikToks with ramen in October 2020. Little did he know this would

bring him to be featured in this cookbook, land him on TV twice, and inspire multiple articles about his work. It just goes to show that you can achieve anything if you put your mind to it!
Baked Feta Ramen 75
Ramen Lasagna 93

@renes.cravings
Rene Subash, also known as Rene's Cravings, loves all things to do with food and cooking! Being from an Indian household, eating and cooking are very important social traditions in Indian culture. She believes that a good hearty meal has the power to bring people together.
Butter Chicken Pasta 85
Chicken 65 Biryani 94

@rootedinspice
For Chaheti, rootedinspice started as a creative outlet to have outside of her 9-to-5, but it quickly turned into a deep passion for bringing awareness to the actual dishes made in South Asian homes—the ones rarely found on the menus of Western restaurants. Admittedly, Chaheti has no professional culinary training (a few years in high school cooking club doesn't count, right?), but she learned to cook intuitively by watching and hearing her mother's techniques and experimenting in the kitchen. While content creation continues to be personally fulfilling for Chaheti, her main goal is that her content can always provide value to her audience—like introducing a lesser-known regional recipe, addressing misconceptions around desi food, or even a tutorial on how to eat with your hands.
Pomegranate Poha 30
Mini Burnt Basque Cheesecakes 153

@scheckeats
Jeremy Scheck is a student at Cornell University double majoring in Spanish and Italian with significant coursework in nutrition, food science, and culinary science. His most popular recipes—crispy potatoes and homemade pasta—have received millions of views.
Strawberry Cream Puffs 150

@sheffara
Ara is a home cook from London who started cooking at the beginning of lockdown in 2020.

Ara loves to binge-watch shows like *Hell's Kitchen* and *MasterChef* UK, where he learns skills and techniques. He spends his weekends hosting friends and family for juicy burgers with triple-cooked fries or some fresh hand-rolled sushi.
Fish and Chips Tortillas 106

@shreyacookssss
The philosophy behind Shreya's Kitchen has always been to foster a community focused on food and body positivity, cultural acceptance, and creating a space for people of all skill levels and interest areas to learn more about easily creating their favorite foods at home.
Extra-Cheesy Grilled Cheese 65

@spiritedla
Hannah believes a well-made cocktail makes life more fun. She pairs cocktail recipes and techniques with fashion, etiquette tips, and history to help people make the most of their drinking experiences.
Cider Rum Punch 173
Large-Batch Bourbon, Peach, and Ginger Arnold Palmer 177

@tazxbakes
To Taz, baking, cooking, and creating content is a form of therapy, a way to project her creativity, and a way to consistently challenge herself. Through it, she's been blessed with the opportunity to share all that she knows with others, and ultimately, she is able to learn from them.
Chocolate-Fudge Baked Oats 40
Crispy Baklava Rolls 146

@theemoodyfoody
Fabrizio Villalpando is a Mexican American self-taught home cook, who prides himself on being an advocate for "comfy cooking" and living leisurely. Known for his soothing ASMR-style videos, Fabrizio's main goal is to show fellow home cooks worldwide, regardless of skill level, how simple it can be to enjoy both casual and fine dining at home.
Chilaquiles Rojos 21

@thegoldenbalance
Ahmad Alzahabi, also known as the Golden Balance, is a Syrian American Muslim who lives

in Michigan. His unique journey and experiences with the culinary world helped him launch his TikTok account and become one of the leading creators, amassing an audience of millions who share a passion for storytelling and food.
Parmesan Garlic Chicken Wings 97

@thekoreanvegan
Joanne Molinaro, a lawyer by trade, started her TikTok account during the summer of 2020. Since then, she has shared her Korean vegan recipes with millions of people while also sharing stories about her family. She is also a cookbook author, long-distance runner, and published poet.
The Ultimate Breakfast Sandwich 28
Kkanpoong Tofu Tacos 73

@thelucasassis_
Lucas is a well-versed bartender who loves telling stories and has a thirst for knowledge of cocktails and craft spirits from around the world. He was born and raised in Brazil but through marriage and travel he fell in love with Mexico's culture, food, and, of course, agave spirits.
The Brazilian Mariachi 172
My Classic Paloma 174

@the_pastaqueen
Nadia Caterina Munno, aka the Pasta Queen, has pasta in her blood. Her family, known in Rome, Italy, as the "Macaronis," has been making pasta and wine in their own factory since the early nineteenth century. As a fifth-generation "Macaroni," Nadia shares her family's secrets with her own special flair.
The Pasta Queen's Tips for Pasta Perfection 81

@theres.food.at.home
August owns John's Juice and Fluffy's NYC, two food businesses in New York City. August's goal is to help level up her audience's relationship with cooking at home, to make it fun and nonintimidating.
Apple Pie Tarts 145

@thesweetimpact
Fan-favorite cake artist Robert Lucas, also known as the Sweet Impact, only started baking one and a half years ago. He is known for his fantastical artistry, modeling cakes after pop culture icons, and more. His very first cake was a unicorn, based on a photo he saw online. He currently resides in Georgia and works as a full-time IT professional.
Fudgy Brownies 142

@thewoksoflife
The Woks of Life is a multigenerational family food blog. Bill, Judy, Sarah, and Kaitlin Leung—father, mother, and daughters (older and younger sisters, respectively)—record their family's history by sharing food and stories. Together they make Chinese cooking easy for millions of home cooks.
Pantry Goals with the Woks of Life 132

@tillyramsay
Tilly Ramsay isn't just Gordon's Ramsay's daughter, she's also known for her CBBC cooking show *Matilda and the Ramsay Bunch*, and has appeared on countless programs like *Strictly Come Dancing*, *MasterChef: Celebrity Australia*, and many more. Though only in her first year in university, Tilly still has time to dance up a storm and make fun of her dad on TikTok.

@twincoast
Ashley and Taylor Johnston are sisters from Vancouver, Canada. They created Twin Coast as a collaborative brand combining their passions for healthy recipes and lifestyle and more!
Vegan Coconut Vanilla Smoothie Bowls 33

@usajalandhar
Mohinder Sareen has been cooking since he was fifteen, when he learned from his dad, who was a chef in both India and the United States. Cooking is his passion and he loves to create and share his recipes.
Crispy, Spiced Fish Pakoras 59

@zaynab_issa
Zaynab Issa is a cook, recipe developer, writer, and freelance creative based in New York. Most recently, Zaynab has designed, written, and published the zine-style cookbook *Let's Eat*, a collection of East African and Indian recipes from her childhood.
Cinnamon Streusel Coffee Cake 42
Classic Tomato Soup 66

index

Note: Page references in *italics* indicate photographs.

Ebury Press, an imprint of Ebury Publishing
20 Vauxhall Bridge Road,
London, SW1V 2SA

Ebury Press is part of the Penguin Random House
group of companies whose addresses can be found
at global.penguinrandomhouse.com

Copyright © 2022 by TikTok
Photography copyright © 2022 by Lauren Volo

First published in the United States of America
by Clarkson Potter in 2022
This edition first published in the United Kingdom
by Ebury Press in 2022

www.penguin.co.uk

A CIP catalogue record for this book is available from
the British Library

ISBN: 9781529148619

Photographer: Lauren Volo
Food Stylist: Monica Pierini
Prop Stylist: Maeve Sheridan
Prop Stylist Assistant: Tsering Dolma
Food Stylist Assistant: Claire Pellegrino
Digital Tech: Christina Zhang
Recipe Testers: Scott Hocker, Rémy Robert,
Grace Rosanova
Editorial Director: Raquel Pelzel
Writer: Emily Stephenson
Editorial Support: Sahara Clement
and Bianca Cruz
Designer: Robert Diaz

Production Editor: Joyce Wong
Production Manager: Derek Gullino
Composition: Merri Ann Morrell
Copy Editor: Kate Slate
Indexer: Elizabeth Parson
Marketer: Stephanie Davis
Publicist: Natalie Yera
Cover design by Robert Diaz
Cover photographs by Lauren Volo

Photography Credits
Alex Guarnaschelli | @guarnaschelli | Johnny Miller
Chelsey White | @chelsweets | Gaby Deimeke
Gabrielle Reyes | @onegreatvegan | Ace Anderson
Giada De Laurentiis | @giadadelaurentiis | Kristin Teig
Gordon Ramsay | @gordonramsayofficial | Mike Irving
h woo lee | @hwoo.lee | Chris Cho
Lucas Assis | @thelucasassis_ | Robiee Ziegler
My Nguyen | @myhealthydish | JBJ Pictures
Nadia Zimmatore | @thepastaqueen | Felix Kunze
Tilly Ramsay | @tillyramsay | Justin Mandel

Printed and bound in Italy by L.E.G.O. S.p.A.

The authorised representative in the EEA
is Penguin Random House Ireland, Morrison Cham-
bers, 32 Nassau Street, Dublin D02 YH68.

Penguin Random House is committed to a sustain-
able future for our business, our readers and our
planet. This book is made from Forest Stewardship
Council® certified paper.

In celebration of the publication of *As Cooked on
Tiktok* in the USA, TikTok has made a donation to No
Kid Hungry, whose mission is to connect kids in need
with the nutritious food they need to grow and thrive.